Dan:
Watch out for d
sneaky mo-fo's. Just ~~
advice for reading my book. Enjoy!

Jim Madonna

A.K.A. Jimmy
Beatboxxx

Poetry from the Next Room

by JIM MADONNA

DORRANCE
PUBLISHING CO
EST. 1920
PITTSBURGH, PENNSYLVANIA 15222

The contents of this work, including, but not limited to, the accuracy of events, people, and places depicted; opinions expressed; permission to use previously published materials included; and any advice given or actions advocated are solely the responsibility of the author, who assumes all liability for said work and indemnifies the publisher against any claims stemming from publication of the work.

Dorrance Publishing Co.
701 Smithfield Street Pittsburgh, PA 15222
Visit our website at www.dorrancebookstore.com

ISBN: 978-1-4809-0184-1
eISBN: 978-1-4809-0454-5

Dedication

In loving memory of

Grandma Sophie Bade
Aunt Nancy Harris

You shall both live on in love.

Although you did not live to see me succeed in having this first book of my poetry published, I have faith that you always believed in my abilities, and each day I think of you both cheering me on from heaven.

My Deepest Appreciation

To all of my friends, teachers, mentors, random acquaintances, and especially my immediate family members, thank you, thank you, and THANK YOU from the bottom of my heart for all of the support you've shown me throughout my relatively short writing career. Whether it was laughing at the funny stuff, contemplating the deeper stuff, or patiently listening to the back-story rants for my darker stuff, I thank the Lord my God for all of your encouraging words, and even the words of discouragement when the power of my pen threatened to harm another person emotionally. I have long believed that everything in this world happens for a reason, and that reason is God's divine and everlasting love expressed through friends and family. To that end, I believe that God gave me both my writing ability and the love of people supporting it so that I could get to the point of where I am today, confidently using my words and writing to inspire others who need it most.

Contents

Poems from High School

(2003-2006)

MY DOWNFALL

Obsession, like chains,
Binds me
Countless days, through and through,
To be perfect,
And yet I know I am not.
I long to escape
Yet I cannot
Because of the pressure
Which I put on my back
Like a heavy backpack filled with books;
Every day
It mounts more and more, but from no outside force
Except me, the inner me,
And will continue to be
−Because of my overwhelming desire
To be the best one they know−
A problem for me:
My downfall.

THE OTHER SIDE

I sit outside the door,
Body frozen, eyes fixed on the clock,
Watching minutes tick by,
Waiting...for what?
Though I knew and know much still,
This I cannot yet grasp:
Why I sit here
Waiting...for what?
Minutes become hours, hours become days,
Yet still I sit
Patiently, for a part of me lingers
Waiting...for what?
Am I waiting for the world to end?
For true love's first kiss?
Should I achieve anything sitting here?
Waiting...for what?
The door opens; I am beckoned inside
To a world of beauty and wonder,
Where happiness lives while sorrows die;
Now I know why I sat here,
Watching and waiting
For the door to open,
So I could see what I always wanted to see:
The other side.

A HOLE TOO DEEP

Just a little white lie
Breaks the crust of the earth
Only a little,
But add a bit more dirt,
And the hole grows
More and more
So that I cannot get out;
Perhaps I have dug
Deeper than I should,
Or deeper, at least,
Further than I needed to dig,
But deep enough for me to see
That lying will not help but only hurt,
And only makes any hole you dig
A hole too deep.

A MESSAGE TO THOSE WHO
DRINK AND DRIVE

Have one drink, then two,
Later losing count;
Get in your car, start the engine,
Meander your way home:
You are drunk.
A light enters your path,
Blinding you before it crushes you.
When you awake,
Only darkness can be seen
As those you love cry;
Try as you might, they cannot be consoled,
And you realize that you are no more
Because of your decision
—Like so many others before you—
To drink and drive.

NATURE'S CHANGING

A sky clear and blue, sun shining bright
Shows nature to be completely alive;
But once clouds come, driving the sun to flight,
The creatures all flee, knowing rain to arrive.

The clouds roll in, what a sight to behold
As the sky grows dark with cascading rain;
The air is electric, the wind is cold,
The unsheltered beasts all endure nature's pain.

Thunder, lightning crashes are heard in the sky,
Brewing up a storm through which all must wait.
Rainbows appear, driving the wild storm to fly;
The sun is back, guarding nature at his gate.

MY MOST TERRIFYING DREAM

Late one night,
Restlessly tossing and turning,
I dreamed of a future
With everyone gone,
And only me to carry on
In the dark and silent world;
A world ravaged by death
Which I had somehow escaped;
I wander through it all,
Noticing homes and stores;
These once stood tall,
But are now shadows of the past.
I call out the names
Of people I once knew,
Growing panicked, running through town,
Hearing only silence;
My only hope of escaping
Is to scream, and in doing so,
Wake up in my own bed.
I glance around, breathing relief,
Knowing how lucky I am
To live in my life,
Instead of what my conscience construed
As my most terrifying dream.

BENEATH THE SURFACE

Trapped, unable to move,
Yet appearing unalarmed;
All the while
Screaming silently
To be let out of my prison
As the world goes on around me:
This image I give myself
—Like the world's expectations—
It seems to enslave me.
Though I am told otherwise,
That I should try to conform
And become perfect,
It is difficult for me to understand.
For deep in my inner being
Another side exists,
Wanting to break free
From this same boring life
On the outside,
Where I am seen
By everybody else
But hidden, all the same,
Beneath the surface.

HERE'S TO THE FUTURE

I wish to take notice
Of what may be,
For acquaintances and friends
Whom I currently see;

We should all come and gather
To remember the now,
Knowing we are all connected
In a purpose, somehow;

Through good times and bad,
As with happiness and pain;
In pulling together
We survived through the rain.

So step up to the table,
Grab a glass and say, "Cheers!"
And salute the unknown
With its hopes and its fears:

Here's to the future,
For whatever it appears.

THE THINGS YOU SAY

Hey, friend,
I see you every day
Smiling your same smile;
But is there more to that smile,
Is there more than what you want me to see?
It is not that I have not known you
Very long,
More like I do not know you
Very well, although
You are always kind to me.
Forgive me, but it seems
There are gaps in everything
I am told.
However, I cannot judge,
Because of my willingness to trust you, so
You can fully accept me.
All the while, the most important rule is forgotten,
Of friendship being based on
Truth and forgiveness;
Realize, good friend of mine,
It is not good, not at all,
To leave gaps unfilled
In everything you do,
As you do with the things you say.

A FACE IN THE CROWD

I see her passing by,
Undoubtedly
On her way somewhere;
For she walks with a purpose
Every day past my window,
Never looking up to see
I am smiling at her.
It is obvious
That she has not the time for flirting,
Or even merely
Chatting over hot cocoa as
She awaits her day's beginning.
She wants to know me,
As I would her;
But there is a barricade existing between us:
It separates loneliness and love.
If she could slow down
For a moment,
My cries to her would be known.
She might see a lover
Bringing her joy:
Until then,
I will only be
A face in the crowd.

ONCE UPON A TIME

Back in the day,
We were young and free,
Creating adventure
Wherever it was needed;
Not a care was paid
To the inevitable passage of time
Until it was upon us,
Forcing us to grow up;
We had to face the world.
The innocence was lost,
As growing up
Exposed us to cold, cruel reality
That happily ever after
Is not always real;
How easy it would be
To go back in time,
Re-experiencing that carefree age
Of youthful innocence,
When life could be taken lightly,
Once upon a time.

THIS IS THE DAY

The time has come
For putting aside
All petty problems and fears
Confining me,
And break out
So that I may show the world
What I'm made of.
Gone are the days
When I would let my faults
Decide my worth;
I must
Step out beyond borders
Ignorantly decided by the world
To be my limits:
You see, I am more, much more,
I am more capable than you say I am.
And I will make this clear, for
It cannot be stopped.
Today is my day to shine;
This is the day.

SHAME ON YOU
(An Anti-Suicide Poem)

I look down, deep into the casket,
Upon the young man
Taken away from life too soon;
Why did you do it?
It should not have ended this way.
There had been people willing to listen;
You did not give them a chance.
In that deep depression
You could not see
Light was at the end of the tunnel.
People say you were wrong
Like they said about you countless times before,
Leading up to your horrible decision,
But I forgive you.
I still feel pain;
Pain etched forever on my heart,
Never to go away,
All because you never loved yourself
Like they all did;
Nobody wanted you to leave.
Suicide is not the only way out of pain, for
Your death killed part of me:
Shame on you.

TELEVISIONATION

The things you see
On your TV
Will influence your mind;
In cartoon jokes
And phony folks
You'll leave your world behind,
Going someplace
Like outer space
Where you'll begin to feel
Your life's a bore,
So you crave more
Of seeing the unreal:
Soon you'll forget
Beyond the set,
Through channels you may flip,
There's more to life
Beyond the strife
That sets your mind to slip.
Drop that remote,
Get out, promote
Skills in communication;
Then you'll be free
By some degree
From televisionation.

EMPTY SHELL

There are times when I feel
I should speak out,
But I know that I cannot.
It is all because of you:
You are always the first one
Deciding my mind;
And if I say anything different,
No mind is paid.
Stop trying to rule my existence,
As you already control
My clothes I wear, my musical tastes,
My very mannerisms;
You may think
Your restrictive love is helping me,
Although it is only
Repressing my spirit,
Causing me to yearn for freedom
In my soul,
So I may no longer feel like
I am an empty shell.

HOLDING SIGNS

You may have wondered why
Each and every Friday
Of every week
I stand in the same hallway
Holding signs:
Sometimes, I also wonder why.
Although I could be
Filling my time in other ways,
I always choose
To arm myself with advice
So that I may brighten the days
Of my fellow peers;
Mind you,
I did not find this sign-advice
Myself, although
I feel from the goodness of my soul
It is my duty
In bringing cheer to others
Needing uplift and laughter
By holding signs.

I WON'T CHANGE FOR YOU

Sometimes I don't make any sense,
And don't know where to go.
Sometimes you can't accept this;
You say it cannot be so.

Most oftentimes I wonder at
Why you are so confused
About how I don't use my mind;
You say it is misused.

I always tried to make you proud,
And did my level best;
Though often when I failed at this,
Your patience ran the test,

I'm sorry if I let you down,
But you will never see
That I will grow to be much more
Than goals you set for me.

Stop worrying about my life,
It simply will not do;
I am an individual,
And I won't change for you.

FALLING DOWN

Roaming freely,
Young life in search of luster,
Standing alone,
Trying to understand
The chip above my shoulder;
I cannot move,
For the weight of past memories;
I'm crying out
To a world that won't listen:
When will I be set free?
This mold I've come to know
Is suffocating me,
And I start to lose my balance,
Clinging desperately
At my one crutch in this life,
My writing, my outlet;
It keeps me from
Falling down.

THEY'LL NEVER HAVE TO KNOW
(An Anti-Smoking Poem)

Come and have a cigarette,
Only one smoke will do;
You won't become addicted
If all you have are two.

Your body will not suffer,
Lung cancer is a myth;
No hospital you'll die in
If you just take a whiff.

Your clothes will start to smell, but
You'll like it soon enough.
Ignore your friends' reactions;
They have not tried the stuff.

Let's keep it all a secret
And start this habit slow;
Just go ahead and take one,
They'll never have to know.

TO FEEL PAIN

When you bully others
It brings you a sense of power and satisfaction,
Only because
You were never a victim yourself.
In surrounding yourself
With other such people,
An aura of unpleasantness emerges.
But in your blindness
To the injustice ever inflicted
By your hand,
You conveniently forgot
The side of things I am forced to see:
Remember,
No one is impervious
From knowing
What it is like
To feel pain.

HOLE IN MY HEART

I think of you, and then I wonder:
Where did we fall out?
I loved you,
Or was that a dream?
The times we shared together
Filled my heart,
My body, my soul,
Everything I was;
Then it was gone.
Just like burning candles,
You extinguished my flame,
Before
Leading me on,
Leaving me lost,
Only to laugh about it;
I drowned in my own tears,
Resurfaced, realizing
You've done this to other guys.
All I have left is
This hole you've burrowed in me:
A hole in my heart.

NO TIME TO BREATHE

I hear the clocks ticking
Without end,
In constant reminder
Of time running out,
Running down,
Trying to keep up with the world;
It never stops.
Wait for me!
Bells ring and buzzers ding,
Hustling me along
So I can bumble at a set pace
Laid down by others,
Causing stress,
Enslaving me to routine;
The older generation already conformed.
Is this necessary?
I must relax, instead of
Running and running,
Leaving myself with
No time to breathe.

MY ANGUISH, MY CURSE

Every day,
I face myself for what I am,
Feeling angry
At my incompetence;
They say I should learn from
Mistakes I routinely commit,
But there are too many
To climb out of, as
I stand neck-deep in my own stupidity
Glaring out at everyone;
They can escape.
Crushed under the weight of being
Socially and functionally inept,
As certain others imply that I am,
I must wonder
Whether it is not society's fault
But mine,
Forcing my faults to handicap me,
So I can hold blame for
My anguish, my curse.

I REALLY COULD BE WORSE
(An Ode to Lack of Social Skills)

I seem quite oblivious
As you can plainly see;
I may not find romance
Until I'm ninety-three!

You can call me stupid,
Dumber than they come;
I often eat the wrapper
Before I chew the gum!

My manners are atrocious,
Just ask my mom and dad;
I badly need improvement,
My habits drive them mad!

I slobber while I'm talking,
My every word's a bleep;
My mind is mostly hollow,
I always oversleep.

I think pain is funny,
I'm one messed-up dude;
I sneeze upon my peers
(Though it is clearly rude).

I fart out loud in public,
And burp without a care;
The things I talk about
Are impolite to share;

Correction seems unlikely,
To others I'm a curse:
But all things considered,
I really could be worse!

MAKE IT CLEAR

You lay down the law
Others are expected to follow,
Including myself;
But when you will not hear me out,
It annoys me.
Somehow it is always up to me
To look out for my friends,
Trying to care, as
They cannot be bothered.
I play the yes-man,
Listening, trying to add up
For what others lack:
It is impossible.
Whatever I try to do correctly
Will not matter
Unless my friends make effort to do likewise;
Rules should be followed,
And I intend to do so.
All you need to do for me is to
Make it clear.

FOUND MY INSPIRATION

I woke early in the morning,
And could not sleep a wink;
As I was drowning in the blues,
I tried to sit and think.

I sat down and started writing,
But my thoughts had run dry;
It seemed I had been defeated,
Until my friend came by:

She said, "Hey now, don't you worry."
I soon stopped feeling blue.
When my good friend had gone away,
I knew what I should do.

I went out and started walking,
Yes, walked more than a mile;
When I found what I was searching,
All I could do was smile.

Now I found my inspiration;
In trouble or in pain,
I can always talk to my friends
If I lose it again.

THE NEVER-ENDING ROAD

One day, I asked myself:
"What is fate?"
Fate, like so many autumn leaves,
Starts by falling off a tree;
This tree is birth.
It is different for everyone,
Blowing them,
Scattering them in every direction;
Their decisions are their only guide.
Ill-made choices bring evil, as
Good will bring good.
For anyone,
Their fate and mine, as with death,
Cannot be escaped
Once they have been born;
We try our best,
Making choices,
Hoping to live our lives to the fullest,
Bumbling, following fate along
The never-ending road.

IMAGE OF PERFECTION

You hold mistakes over my head
Committed in my past:
Why?
Nothing I do is
Good enough for you;
My shoulders sag from the weight of expectation.
The stupid things I say,
Dumber things that I do
Drive you crazy;
You say that I am too old,
That I don't think about
What I should be:
Stop nagging!
I'll get better in good time,
I always did.
Give me a chance for once to improve
Before judging me
By the standards of my peer group;
I try, but
I cannot measure up to your
Image of perfection.

FORGIVE MYSELF AT LAST

Your eyes tell the story
Behind your cold expression,
And I begin to worry
About that first impression:

Mistakes in the open
Will cloud your vision of me;
You see the things kept inside
The public can never see.

Failure drives me downward,
A failure of broken trust:
I see deep down you're hurting
From a faith reduced to dust.

It will not be easy,
Since my life has been a lie.
You may not ever trust me,
But I'll make a move to try.

Let's put this behind us,
Out the window, in the past;
I'll show you I am truthful,
Then forgive myself, at last.

JUST ANOTHER DAY

Take a breath, and count to three.
Let your problems fall on me.
Everything may turn to gray,
But it's just another day.
Close your eyes, and look again:
See things different now and then.

Turn your back, and you will fall;
It's all good, you gave your all.
Brace your wits, and face your fear:
See yourself, but not as clear.
Plan a path out in your mind,
Step outside your daily grind.

Get in line, and wait your turn.
There is much you have to learn.
You may lose, but soon you'll win;
Give the world another spin.
Everything may turn to gray,
But it's just another day.

TEARS OF BLOOD
(In Memory of September 11, 2001)

The darkness descended from
An average Tuesday,
Blackened by a senseless attack;
Planes break the morning tranquility,
Exploding, as
Bodies rain from the sky.
Proud towers crumble, more are dead.
Elsewhere, other innocent people are forced to suffer;
Somewhere, a dictator laughs.
Here, there is only sorrow, as
Families cry;
They are victims of terror born from hatred.
Over the years since,
One brave leader fought to protect us,
Forced to play the hero;
Now people seem to forget his role.
Today, from patriotism springs
A proud, strong America as
Wounds heal, leaving visible scars;
These may never completely heal.
We know
Terror must be vanquished, otherwise
Future generations may still cry tears of blood.

I ONLY WANT A TRIM

Just a trim is all I need
To put my hair in place;
Just a trim is all I need
So you can see my face.

No shaved head or crew cut, please;
They make my head look round.
Shorter here, a lock cut there,
My hair is on the ground.

I do not want a Mohawk,
Nor spikes stuck in the air;
As long as it is simple,
I really do not care.

No fancy foreign hairdos;
They're really hard to clean.
If you need to dye my hair
Just please, don't dye it green.

I don't want streaks in my hair,
But now it seems so grim:
Why so hard to understand
I only want a trim?

THE MATCHES WILL BURN

Where is all the rain?
This heat is just too much to take.
Relieve all my pain,
Before I crumble up and break.

The matches will burn;
The fire spins out of control.
No ashes to turn;
There's nothing left inside this hole.

The judge turns his head;
The jury takes its own sweet time.
The verdict is read;
You're branded guilty of this crime.

This lesson you'll learn:
Don't take the laws into your hand.
No need for concern;
Not everyone can understand.

No need for concern.
This lesson you'll learn.
No ashes to turn.
The matches will burn.

FEELING THIS WAY

Another day goes by,
Worse than yesterday,
As I feel my self-esteem unraveling
Because of people I know,
Or used to think I cared about knowing.
I wish
They would just stop
Their sugar-coated insults to see
The human inside
This worn and befuddled body;
I have feelings,
So do you.
How I wish I fit into their puzzle,
Instead of being
Good enough for insult, but not enough for respect.
Now that I see their scheme,
I want to ignore it
So maybe it will go away, and I can stop
Feeling this way.

MAKE IT UP TO YOU

I want you to know right now,
I'll never apologize
For things I said so long ago,
And all the things I did;
I never said
I wouldn't try,
But it's too late to move on.
It never had to get
This way, but here I am,
Down on my knees,
Begging you, please
Try to let your issues with me fall.
This will never work
Without tearing us apart;
I know this can't be right,
But I will never
Bring myself down, so I can
Make it up to you.

AUTUMN LEAVES

The leaves glint in the sun,
Glimmering, shimmering,
Blowing in the breeze,
Coming together as one
Big, beautiful mosaic of colors,
Providing peace
But only for a short while;
Eventually, they lose their luster.
The leaves fall on the ground,
Dampened by rain,
Fading into the earth;
Soon, the beauty is all gone.
Now,
It is only a burden.
The beauty of autumn is
So short,
But for a moment
There is no greater majesty
Than Nature's greatest painting:
Autumn leaves.

MEANINGLESS

Time is a river,
Flowing, slowly drifting on
To eternity;
The human race, meanwhile,
Goes through motions
Necessary
For preserving itself;
Fighting wars,
It tries vainly to make its mark.
Through the violence, we can see scars,
Really mere cuts;
History passes them by.
The center of the universe
Belongs
Not to us, but to
A higher power somewhere else;
We think
Everything we do is important.
But, in the end, is it all
Meaningless?

DEAL WITH THIS AGAIN

It feels like everyone
Wants to get inside my head;
Take away
What you can,
Until privacy is dead;
I cannot understand,
What do you want from me?
Make or break,
It's all a fake,
This is not what I want to be.
Let it go.
It always feels like
I'm always wrong, not right;
Go break free,
Then you'll know
What it's like
The chains I see,
And you will know you never
Had a doubt that you would ever
Deal with this again.

EVERYTHING IS FINE

Beyond the truth, beyond the lies,
Beyond what lives, beyond what dies,
Beyond the things you feel inside,
Everything is fine.

Beyond the ice, beyond the fires,
Beyond your hopes and deep desires,
Beyond the dreams you swept aside,
Everything is fine.

Beyond the facts you know are there,
Beyond all those too cold to care,
Beyond the thoughts you long to share,
Everything is fine.

Beyond the tasks of each new day,
Beyond the things you do and say,
You will find peace, somewhere, some way;
Everything is fine.

ODD MAN OUT

I can feel the panic starting up again.
I know I knew the reason,
But I can't remember when.
Every day it hurts
And it will never go away,
Dreading I would say the words
I never thought I'd say:

I'm the odd man out,
And I'm alone as I can be.
Go ahead and shout it out,
So I can just be free;
And I never had a doubt;
I'm the odd man out.

I try not to listen to things people say.
I'm living in denial,
But I hear them every day.
Anger reaches boiling point,
But never leaves my lips;
Life becomes a valley
Filled with many drops and dips:

I'm the odd man out,
And I'm alone as I can be.
Go ahead and shout it out,
So I can just be free;
And I never had a doubt;
I'm the odd man out.

Time is just too precious
To get wrapped in deep depression;
It's how we live that traps us;
We determine our direction.
The past is but a burden,
Pinning us down on the ground;
Throw away your anger,
And you'll turn your life around.

I'm the odd man out,
But I'm as happy as can be.
If I was like everyone,
I wouldn't be this free.
And I know what I'm about;
I'm the odd man out.

SICK OF THIS WAITING

Twenty minutes to the end of this class;
I'm sitting here, watching time slowly pass.
I wonder just when the boredom will end,
And I wonder if I'll reclaim my lost friend.

I've been waiting for a year and a day;
Somehow, it's longer with nothing to say.
What happened to all our memories drawn?
We used to talk, but those days are gone.

I'll never know what became of our trust;
Your loyalty was consumed by your lust.
My hopes of you are so quickly deflating,
So much for our love; I'm sick of this waiting.

LOCKED OUT

Turn off these voices in my head, nagging, always questioning;
They say the same things over again, redundantly condescending;
Every biting word is the truth, the problem is never ending.

And I feel locked out from solutions so close, yet so far beyond my reach;
I want to break this trap; I'm tired of these lessons,
I don't practice what I preach.
I feel locked out.

Your caring takes me off the edge when I know I'm drowning;
Yet I will not admit the truth if my doubts are dawning;
Will you just get off my back? There's no room for improving.

And I feel locked out from solutions so close, yet so far beyond my reach;
I want to break this trap; I'm tired of these lessons,
I don't practice what I preach.
I feel locked out.

I'm tired of this feeling I should be concealing,
When my heart is bleeding from efforts misleading;
I'll be perfect someday, and then you will not say
You're still locked out.

SPEAK OUT

I'm sick of all the war, so many people crying;
And everything's a mess, so many people dying;
The system doesn't care about the people left behind.
I know not everyone is blind; it's such a grind.

Young people trapped by oppression,
Speak out, it's your given right!
Speak out for what you believe in;
Speak out with all your might!

I'm sick of this routine, it's getting so redundant.
My work's not recognized, so now I feel despondent;
They say I'll never see what all the other people know.
I'll never make it in the show, so here I go.

Young people trapped by frustration,
Speak out, it's your given right!
Speak out for what you believe in;
Speak out with all your might!

No one can keep you down or break you down to shame,
If you believe what you're about;
Nothing can ever change that is forced to stay the same.
You can decide, if you speak out.

RUNNING IS FUN, EATING IS NEAT

I like to run.
Running is fun.
Running is fun when you run in the sun.
Running is fun if you've only begun,
Until you are done;
Then sit and relax and eat meat on a bun.

I like to eat.
Eating is neat.
Eating is neat when you eat in a seat.
Eating is neat if you eat lots of meat.
But woe, if you cheat,
You'll soon grow so big that you can't see your feet!

EVERY TIME

When I look at you,
I'm reminded of the seasons;
Each one is different,
All are beautiful in their own right.
Do you still love me?
Years away,
Will you be there to turn on the lights?
Never doubt tomorrow will come,
And we can be together.
This love of mine burns like that rose
You gave me;
Then I found the thorns.
I'm hurt.
Soon enough, I overcome it.
Love can be so inconsistent.
Do you feel the same?
Why do you always make this so confusing?
Always, you
Throw me for a loop,
And it tickles me every time.

CHANGE THE WORLD
Song/Poem

Days go by, wars are raging.
People cry, nothing's changing.
Try to ask, there's no explaining.
You can't mask the problems gaining.

Go change the world, reach out, you will see
Life can be good, as it used to be.
Nothing is easy in life to achieve;
You'll change the world, but you must believe.

Things will die, no one's caring.
Don't ask why, no kindness sparing.
Start to care, life looks better.
Hope is there, so don't forget her.

Don't give up if the world puts you down;
Change isn't easy to accept.
Make a smile from what once was a frown;
Clean up the tears the world has wept.
Plans for the future must yet be unfurled,
So change the world.

OVERRATED

You said I only care when I want to,
I only do what I have to.
You said I never listened to reason,
I always change with the season.

You're overstated when you can't get to the point;
So complicated, I just can't get over you.
Too motivated, and you just don't realize
It's overrated.

They said what you do will never matter,
One day all your dreams will shatter.
They said no one else will ever listen,
It's like living in a prison.

I don't care if you won't dare
To make up your mind, go leave them all behind.
Why does it hurt? I'm feeling like dirt.
You hide behind the shame, the lies bleed down your shirt.

You're overstated when you can't get to the point;
So complicated, I just can't get over you.
Too motivated, and you just don't realize
It's overrated.

SO NERVOUS

"Jim has the floor,"
I hear the speaker say.
Sweating, I rise, walking toward the podium.
It seems so far away.
My hands, cold and clammy,
Shake now more than before.
Everyone stares at me.
Why do they insist on being difficult?
Stop it!
I have reached the podium;
My turn comes to speak.
Word form,
Never reaching my mouth as
My face turns red;
It's like this every time I laugh,
But no one is laughing.
Judge not
How eloquently I may speak;
I cannot live up to expectations
When
I'm so nervous.

UNRECOGNIZED TALENT

O, destroyers of my dreams,
Trample my battered hopes
To the ground!
You do not care about the
Struggling artist,
Favoring the names of those
Already written in stone;
Disenfranchise my spirit more,
Building the blocks
Of pretended future success,
Only so
You can break me down.
Curse your shallow preferences,
Condemning my
Soul to solitude, sorrow, sadness, and shame!
Left in darkness,
I feel nothing but emptiness.
Give me a chance,
Foul pretenders,
So the shell of invisibility may be broken,
Revealing my
Unrecognized talent.

COMING HOME

Late one night,
By the starry light,
I was making my way
When I heard voices say:
"They've moved on without you."
A tear rolled down
And hit the ground,
Knowing what it could be
That bothered me;
I had also moved on, too.

So, I'm coming home,
After wandering
And wondering
Why I ever thought of leaving
If there's nothing I'm achieving
As I roam;
Yes, now I know that
I'm coming home.

No one knows
Why the cold wind blows
So much stronger when
You're without a friend;
Then the wind will take you.
Look up above,
And know there's love;
Even if you feel cold,
Life will unfold,
And your world begins anew.

Soon, you're coming home,
After wandering
And wondering
Why you ever thought of leaving
If there's nothing you're achieving
As you roam;
Yes, before you know,
You're coming home.

ANOTHER DAY I'LL STAY IN BED

Another day in this routine life,
Another thorn to cause me strife,
Another test I'm forced to take,
Another stress I have to fake,
Another chance I've thrown away,
Another reason I must stay,
Another honor for another face,
Another chance for another race,
Another saying or another quote,
Another pointless anecdote,
Another hero for another age,
Another way to cage the rage,
Another new guilt for another crime,
Another thing to pass the time,
Another mistake with no excuse,
Another reason for abuse,
Another fad that may never fly,
Another time to wonder why,
Another chance it's in my head,
Another day…I'll stay in bed.

NOTHING TO SAY

The day she left me started out like any other day,
No signs that life would ever change in any other way;
She told me she was leaving soon, but be that as it may
I stood there, staring awkwardly with nothing I could say.

She was the one thing that mattered, but everything was shattered
When she walked away;
Now everything is wrong and it's been that way too long:
There's nothing to say.

Within a week, I heard rumors she'd hooked up with my friend.
With him, that day, I picked a fight, which I could not defend,
And my sorrow reached the point where my world was at an end;
So much confusion in my life, so much, I could not mend.

It's been too wrong for much too long,
But she's been gone, so I moved on.

She was the one thing that mattered, but everything was shattered
When she walked away;
Now everything is wrong and it's been that way too long:
There's nothing to say.

MYCELIUM

The anxiety comes slowly,
Creeping through me
Spreading in my brain like mycelium
Of some deadly fungus;
In growing,
It becomes unstoppable.
It has no reason.
It has no face.
The purpose of this panic is unclear, as
It comes and goes.
Never leaving,
The shadows of panic torment me.
Mycelium weaves
A tangled web of mushrooms,
Opening to fearful confusion;
Unlike mushrooms, it cannot be killed.
Striking without warning,
More spores are spun;
Fear spreads.
You can kill one mushroom,
But still,
There will be mycelium.

BREAKDOWN AVENUE

I failed the test, and then lost the quest;
I'm stressing in my brain.
I lost the girl, and down came my world;
I don't mean to complain.
This life I live, there's too much I give.
It's driving me insane.

So once again I'll take a walk down Breakdown Avenue;
Don't worry if I'm on the edge, it's really nothing new.
My mind is blank, I feel washed out, there's nothing I can do;
It's all the same on Breakdown Avenue.

I broke the pact with the cards I stacked;
They're crashing on the floor.
I gave it all, but I took a fall;
It seems she wanted more.
I have no doubt what she is about;
She threw me out her door.

So once again I'll take a walk down Breakdown Avenue;
Don't worry if I'm on the edge, it's really nothing new.
My mind is blank, I feel washed out, there's nothing I can do;
It's all the same on Breakdown Avenue.

ESCAPE FROM THIS TODAY

My stomach is full, but I can't stop eating.
I should exercise, but I can't stop cheating.
I know what I should do,
But I don't have a clue!
I know my weight repulses you;
I ate more than I could chew.

It's time for a diet; I know I need to try it.
Just so I can escape from this, I'll escape from this.
I don't need a riot, since I don't really buy it.
I just want to escape from this; I'll escape from this today.

My mind is too full, but I can't stop thinking.
I'm trying to swim, but I just keep sinking.
I don't know what to do.
I think I'm turning blue!
And I bet I really missed my cue;
I'll fix what I know is true.

It's time for a diet; I know I need to try it.
Just so I can escape from this, I'll escape from this.
I don't need a riot, since I don't really buy it.
I just want to escape from this; I'll escape from this today.

STILL A THOUSAND MORE

A thousand times I've lived and died,
A thousand times I've almost cried.
A thousand times I've fallen down,
A thousand times I've been a clown.

A thousand times I've lost my cool,
A thousand times I've been a fool.
A thousand times I've flipped my top,
A thousand times I've tried to stop.

A thousand times I've felt like slime,
A thousand times I've lost my rhyme.
A thousand times I've longed to share,
A thousand times I've tried to care.

A thousand times I've been torn up
By inner civil war;
A thousand times I've made it, but
There's still a thousand more.

NOT SO BAD
(On Living with Obsessive-Compulsive Disorder, or OCD)

Every time I lose my cool,
I always feel like such a fool.

Always worry, always stress;
This feeling will only oppress.

My mind goes as I start to lose
My will to care, I cannot choose.

Sometimes it just feels like I
Just want to stop, just want to cry;

Though I know it comes from me,
I can't get out, I can't break free.

OCD is such a bore,
But this is what I can't ignore.

It drags me up, brings me down;
Suffocating, I will drown.

I know it's all in my head,
But make me calm, or life I'll dread!

Every day, I muddle through
And try to think of something new.

I need to end these thoughts inside;
My brain is starting to get fried.

But looking back, I also see
My OCD did much for me.

You see, obsession drove a need:
If I should try, I must succeed.

I worked hard, achieved good grades;
It's true; my effort never fades.

In my time I've gotten far.
Who knows, I could become a star.

I'll find something that I enjoy,
And there, my passion stands ahoy.

I know the success I've had,
So honestly, it's not so bad.

WORTHLESS DESTINY

Day after each mind-numbing day,
I sit and I stare
And try not to care;
The world moves on its merry way.

I always stand far off alone,
Holding up a sign,
I stand out of line;
Inside, my senses bleed and groan.

No matter how hard I may try
To not let them see
How weird I can be,
I'm never just a normal guy.

Every time, broken and stressed,
I fall down and cry,
And each time I die;
Soon, I feel just downright depressed.

Nothing is right when all is wrong;
I lose everything,
Who cares about bling?
I'm way too messed up to belong.

This world is becoming a drag;
It puts me in place,
I try to save face;
Getting kicked, it's pointless to brag.

Though I clean up myself, I see
My shortcomings screwed
This Special-Needs dude;
It's just my worthless destiny.

IT WILL SOON BE GONE

Each day I wake up,
I see the world as it is;
It is cold and strange.

I want greater things.
I wish to do it all, but
Life just holds me back.

I know I'm offbeat.
I feel that there is more here,
I see no choices.

Please don't get me wrong:
I can see your point of view,
I just don't agree.

People are so blind.
Caught up in their little world,
They lose sight of truth.

Time will never show
All the little things we do;
They will not matter.

We have worked so hard,
But what can we show for it?
It will soon be gone.

LIES

Small, unimportant opinions of the masses;
Carry me along, on your shallow-minded nothingness.
I don't care about the majority of empty conformity;
Can't you see I'm bleeding, dying?
I want to live my own life,
Find my own self;
I'm wrapped in the tourniquet of my soul.
This is not another small thing,
Like stupid fads our generation embraces so willingly;
I want the pride of knowing I am my own, without feeling
My Individuality will only crucify me.
Self-worth is a joke, something beyond my decision:
"Be yourself, just like everyone else."
I'm vomiting, getting sick from the black stench of
The "norm" accepted by all.
Minds can be broken, and then you become another victim.
Thinking a thousand ideas, you believe none.
Desensitized, nobody dares speak out.
Well, you can take my image of myself,
Break it and make it your own,
Mask my speech with empty words.
But my spirit is mine, still
It is a slave to nothing,
Especially dirty, phony, REEKING LIES!

LOOKING DOWN FROM ATOP THE CLOUDS

The world…
It seems so significant
Living down below,
Day by day;
It all seems so important.
But now,
Borne upward
On wings made of steel,
As it all falls away from you,
You realize
You are insignificant,
Like those ants you crushed
Last week;
You did not care then.
But from a view
High, high above everyone living
Day by day,
You know
We are the ants, and
God's divine will is all that matters.
And so we fly overhead,
Looking down, from atop the clouds.

THANK YOU FOR YOUR TIME

Trapped inside
This lonely heart of mine,
There's a fire burning faintly to be let out
Every time I self-destruct,
And I scream out silently:
Tell me now,
Just when
Did I become this crazy?
Was it overnight?
Or was it a process in the working?
Tears fall,
Duties call,
And I hurt myself again
Every time I fail;
This existence is nothing at all,
Down into the dark tunnel of my mind
Waiting for light,
I try to fight.
Losing every battle, losing every war;
I can't escape
When my anger closes in,
Wearing away my soul;
Fading, I'm burning out forever;
Thank you for your time.

FRUSTRATION

Every night, I lose sleep
Working hard,
Only to find pointlessness surrounding me;
I tell myself,
"Finally, I will catch a break!"
But yet,
This turns out to be an untruth.
I achieve nothing
Attempting to do everything,
Only causing anxiety;
Wearing me down
To the point of burning out,
But I live to stress for another day,
Falling,
I crash and burn;
Struggling, I complete work
I already did.
Falling out from obligations,
Barely keeping my sanity afloat;
Running toward the wall,
I find no escape.
Now,
I am led to believe there is
No cutting loose from this inevitable frustration.

WAY TOO DEEP

The burnout feeling has begun
Sinking deeper,
Falling faster;
I cannot hide, I cannot run,
Emotions melt into my soul.

The washout feeling never wanes,
Never showing,
Never knowing;
As stress produces aches and pains
A smile stays on, but takes its toll.

I've felt these feelings deep within,
Wearing downward,
Beating inward;
That which was thick is spread too thin,
I hardly find the time to sleep.

I've eaten more than I can chew,
Started choking,
Hence the cloaking,
Hiding what I know to be true;
And now I'm stuck in way too deep.

ANTHEM OF DISGRACE

I'm writing you this poem
As my anthem of disgrace,
So all emotions fade away
And do not leave a trace.

I wish that I could take back
All the stuff I put you through;
But how could I escape myself
As problems only grew?

I tried, failed, and I floundered,
While still, everything got worse.
Yet never knowing what I did,
I fed my endless curse.

Goodbye to all the caring,
And goodbye to all the pain;
In silence I shall leave you with
My tears lost in the rain.

Is anyone still out there?
I do not think I can face
The demons I've created from
My anthem of disgrace.

YOU MADE ME THIS WAY

Waiting until the present burns to black,
I seethe in silence.
You tried to be my friend.
And I wanted a friend, but it wasn't you.
You followed me obsessively, I know you did.
Lied innocently, all so I could entangle myself in your web;
Social death lies within its strands.
How do I say it gently?
I may hurt you like you hurt me unknowingly;
First of all, you're simply weird.
But I helped you, only out of sorrow:
You have no friends, nor ever did.
I can see you are desperate for friendship, though
I know the kind of friendship you offer: It's not normal.
Perhaps, that would explain why you represent
All the social barricades I refuse to know;
True, you have religion,
But that gives you no right to force me
Into your way of thinking:
I don't need the salvation you offer.
Believe me, I am not prejudiced, but I don't like you.
I want you to just go far away from me.
Before you leave, please remember well these words:
You made me this way.

FLY AWAY ON BROKEN WING

Crying, trying,
I claw my way up to the top.
Bumbling, tumbling,
I fall back down, but I can't stop.

Making messes,
I run away from what I've done.
Building stresses,
I lose much more than I have won.

Kissing failure,
I cut my bleeding lips away.
Losing pleasure,
I see achievement lost in gray.

Losing more ground,
I quickly cover up mistakes.
Making no sound,
I beat myself 'till something breaks.

Feeling lowly,
I make myself into nothing.
Dying slowly,
I fly away on broken wing.

ONLY HUMAN

Fix me up,
But I'm broken for good
Still beyond repair;
As I lost my youth,
You lost your hope.
My faults forever shattered
Your illusion of me grown up,
As your smile
—Taking my pride in stride—
Hides your bitter disappointment
Of the young man
You only wish you knew;
You say
I don't think right
—Or is my thinking too slow?
I don't know.
If I were not so obsessive,
I wouldn't even care.
Your logical mind
Can't define
What makes me inept?
Here's a clue:
What does "Asperger Syndrome" mean to you?
Oops, I forgot:
You don't believe in conditions
Or that people simply make mistakes
Like me, like everyone.
Sure, some mistakes are bigger than others,
But don't lose hope:
Some people take longer than others.
Remember,
I am not you.
My level of organization
—Like answers to your questions I find "vague"—
Is far from perfect,
But not all efforts yield results.
I am not being defensive,
I am only human.

I READ IT ANYWAY

I shouldn't read this poem,
No matter what you say;
I shall not read this poem,
Not now, no how, no way!

I shouldn't read this poem,
Knowing what it may do;
I shall not read this poem,
It might just depress you.

I shouldn't read this poem,
It's evil to its core;
I shall not read this poem,
For it is quite a bore.

I shouldn't read this poem,
It's angrier than most;
I shall not read this poem,
Though you'll become engrossed.

I shouldn't read this poem,
But now, I'm sad to say:
Despite my countless efforts,
I read it ANYWAY!

THE SNOWBOARDING FOOL

From "Jimmy's Many School Poems," January 2000, for a sixth-grade poetry project
Readapted January 10, 2006

Oh, he is the Snowboarding King.
He would wear an unlucky white ring.
Through the snow he would dash,
And the ice he would crash,
Then complain about how it would sting.

Oh, he is the Ice Skating Clown.
He could skate without making a sound.
On the ice he would slip,
Over twigs he would trip,
And his howl could be heard all around.

Oh, he is the Ski-Sloping Fool.
He will probably never be cool.
It is only a game,
Do not ask for his name,
For he is the Snowboarding Fool.

PRETEND TO SMILE

As I watch the fires of apathy
Burn down my face in tiny teardrops, I wonder:
Why do I deserve to be invisible?
I crave recognition.
I deserved it, too, this time;
But as always, I got the shaft.
One step ahead for every two steps behind
Every walking image of perfection I follow.
It would never occur to the masses
That other people can be great beyond achievers set in stone;
But I say nothing, knowing
Complaint will only bury my cause.
So I go on, through these everyday repetitions,
Doing my duties as though nothing is wrong;
I try my best, and you actually believe
That I am happy with my burden,
When I wish, desperately,
You would give a hardworking guy a break where
A break is due.
But you only pretend to care, ignoring me,
Omitting me for an unspoken prejudice:
You cover a lie,
You cover with a smile.
Fine, I will play along with your game, as I pretend to smile.

LOST IN THIS WORLD

Hiding beneath this cheerful visage
Lies a little boy,
Scared and confused, unsure
Not only about his future,
But of his heart's desire.
I used to know my dreams like the back of my hand:
−I was going to shake the world!−
But now,
I sit in awkward silence;
Slapped, backhanded by reality:
This is your finest hour,
Isn't it, fate?
Laugh, malicious keeper,
As you build me up, you break me down.
All this is for your own sick, twisted
Absurd amusement:
The little boy has grown up,
What has he grown up for?
His bleeding wings of hope are gone,
Trampled into dust,
And you still see the pleasure of me
Confused, confined, cut short in my prime:
Without a dream,
I am lost in this world.

YOU WOULD NOT HEAR ME SCREAM

You see that I am smiling, so you would not hear me scream.
You see that I am laughing, so you would not hear me scream.

You cannot see I'm lying, so you would not hear me scream.
You cannot see I'm dying, so you would not hear me scream.

You will not see the anguish, so you would not hear me scream.
You will not see me languish, so you would not hear me scream.

You may not solve my problem, so you would not hear me scream.
You may not want to stop them, so you would not hear me scream.

You couldn't stop this feeling, so you would not hear me scream.
You could not stop me keeling, so you would not hear me scream.

You did not let me vent, and so you would not hear me scream.
You did not just relent, and so you would not hear me scream.

You could not end my failing, so you would not hear me scream.
You could not stand my bailing, so you would not hear me scream.

You would not hear me out, because you would not hear me scream.
And now the joke's on you because you would not hear me scream;
Oh, you did not hear me scream; no, you could not hear me scream.

I DON'T CARE

I see beneath your lies,
The reasons fall behind your self-serving needs;
You claim to think you know
The best thing for me,
But I beg to differ,
Knowing the truth existing behind the reality
You want to believe.
In my eyes, this means nothing.
Look at all of my efforts:
They are for you, all and only for you,
Not me.
I only care because you demand it,
Like those people
Claiming the title of "Society";
They demand a perfection of which I am incapable.
This obligation pile of stinking, rotting feces,
Is it not a labor of love, but a chore?
It is an act of self-slavery;
You are the only one who benefits.
You want the truth?
Good, you can have it.
Listen carefully,
Because I hope to say it only once:
I...DON'T...CARE.

BEHIND MY FACE

When you see me,
You see my cheerful countenance,
But is it a real smile you see?
Glass lenses dull the eyes,
Hiding secrets;
More secrets are hidden than
Words can ever tell.
Maybe, the reason I hide,
Wearing my armor
Of happy signs, glasses,
Lies and a smile
Is that
I am protecting you.
That way,
You won't see the real cause
Of my consternation,
And feel need to give me comfort,
Not knowing
It is only me,
My greatest foe oppressing me;
This oppression is not for
Lack of possession,
I have plenty of things.
I do not feel oppressed because
I am ignored;
I have plenty of friends.
This oppression is really from
Fear of self:
I am afraid of my feelings,
Scared of my obsessive tendencies,
Terrified that you won't like me
When you see
I don't drink, smoke,
Huff anything,
Fornicate loosely,
And I believe in God.
My morality,
Which I mask from speaking,
Might scare you;
I know

If you are really my friends,
You will understand.
The truth is that
You don't know me
As you think you do;
And you cannot truly respect me
Until you look deep into my eyes
And see
The unspoken volumes
Written
Behind my face.

POWERLESS

I feel the darkness
Of everyday life descending,
Covering, smothering;
I see the hopelessness of only for now
Becoming only for always;
Nothing ever changes, as
Maximum effort yields minimum results.
As apathy consumes me,
Burning, churning, putting out my flame,
I know this cannot be reversed.
Despite my outward cries, you laugh
As you throw my cries back mockingly,
To hit me in the face;
The bleeding scabs of bad decisions
Never heal, reproducing frustration to
Haunt me, taunt me;
This voice of bother goes to sleep,
But it never completely dies.
I sit in silence, suffering, knowing
I can fight this oppression,
But it will take more hope than I possess;
I distract myself, but I can still see
In shades of inevitable darkest truth
I will always be powerless.

PAIN FOR PLEASURE

The sun is shining, everyone seems at peace.
But not me;
Torn inside, broken by emotion,
I look in on life from an outside world:
I am the outsider.
Despite efforts of joining in, becoming a part of it all,
I am empty; lost from caring
Except when you find in me
One more mean-spirited tasteless joke pulled apart from dignity
To make of me another tool, another of the dancing fools:
What am I?
Unless I am entertaining you, my value becomes intangible,
Threatening obliteration of my senses;
My very worth hangs unbalanced,
Soon to stop my breath, bringing freedom to my soul,
Pulling me out of my abyss;
This empty place I call my own is cascading,
Crumbling, falling inward over onto itself—
Now the light can shine down into my soul,
Fading out the demon lies inside of me,
Cleansing the inward abyss of my mind, my soul, myself;
Filling the empty space, I am whole again.
This inward light comforts me;
It trades my pain for pleasure.

HEADLIGHTS AND HIND SIGHTS
(Dedicated in memory of Athear, Mayada, and Ali Jafar)

Lights bear down
On a lonely stretch of road;
Sounds of screeching
Tires slice through the silence of the night.
Voices cry out;
In the darkness, no one can hear you screaming.
As you slip from this life,
You leave behind
The sad, the broken, the lonely;
Looking back, we felt immortal,
Never thinking
Death could destroy our perfect world,
–Until it became reality.
In retrospect,
We should have known from the beginning
Death would happen,
But we waited
Until our mortality became apparent;
Now, the memories are all we have left.
These are the images of our past,
Seared forever into our souls;
Eventually,
The only memories will be headlights and hind sights.

I WRITE FOR SANITY

These are the words
I write to let everyone see
Inside of me and share how I really feel;
These are the words
I write to love myself,
Despite not being the "perfect weight";
These are the words
I write to hide my emotions
So you would not hear me scream;
These are the words
I write to flip a certain proud finger
In the face of indifference and adversity;
These are the words
I write to show you that
I am not perfect, not even close;
These are the words
I write to have a better outlet
Than hurting people not deserving abuse;
These are the words
I write in order to express
My dark, angry, more depressing thoughts;
These are the words
I write for never-ending days
And long, sleepless nights of insomnia;
These are the words
I write for hard work done
Without pleasure and without reward;
These are the words
I write to banish my inner demons
From clouding me in dense frustration;
These are the words
I write for this unchanging world
Full of people living in monotony;
These are the words
I write for my own peace of mind,
Words that will only fall on deaf ears;
These are the words
I write to gain a small sense of power
From feelings of great powerlessness;
These are the words

I write to transcend a confusing world
And find my own source of understanding;
These are the words
I write for countless reasons
As for many times and seasons;
But these are the words
I write to serve my escape from reality.
These are the words
I write for sanity.

AUTHOR OF MY DESTRUCTION

Dismayed, distraught, distressed,
And disgusted,
I sit here again,
Pondering why everything seems so wrong;
I think I know the reason.
Too long I entrapped myself
In expectation,
Feeling the familiar endless cycle:
Sit down, shut up,
Don't complain, keep smiling,
Do as you are told,
Nothing will matter in the end.
(Please leave all carefree happiness at the doorway,
From this moment,
You'll be overstressed and under slept.)
I'm sick of caring,
So now I feel lost and used up.
Hoping to escape,
All I can do is writing about my feelings, when
Nobody listens to my spoken pain.
My thoughts manifest
In my frustration,
And I know it will be my undoing, as I
Become the author of my destruction.

WALL OF MEMORIES

Silent, smiling pictures
Grace my surroundings,
Adorning the walls of the halls of my mind;
Each is a look into happier times, as
They are from places of carefree belonging.
Why, now,
Can I see only shadows?
Already, they fade to the back of my mind.
Just look at me:
Wiling away an unspoken misery,
Refusing to face myself,
In denial of the real matter at hand:
I have not moved on.
All I see is the forgotten darkness
Of a dead past-self;
Cloaked in pain
Spawning from social inadequacy,
I fear I may never rise above myself to see
I am more than a shadow.
Once I realize my present self,
Only then shall I be free to move along,
Making my future,
Instead of hiding behind my
Wall of memories.

Poems from College

(2006-2010)

AMID THE CONFUSION

Tears stinging, anger burning,
Lies falling faster than rain,
I silently smolder,
Wondering, RAGING at my lack of control:
Why must you protect me?
It only fuels the powerless feeling.
I know the truth:
You only see me as another mindless automaton
Built to serve, and
Take it in the proverbial butt
Like it was meant to be;
But this is wrong…YOU are wrong.
I am always either put in place,
Or a protective embrace,
Just for the sake of this
Same-old, same-old
Shut-up-and-smile mentality of lies;
I can see right through you, to
Your insults bleeding
Pointless confusion;
Hear me: I HAVE A VOICE!
Despite this oppression you call life,
My voice will be heard
Amid the confusion.

PAPER WORDS AND CARDBOARD THOUGHTS

Now, I can safely say that we're falling apart,
My hands clenched, heart racing as I sit here, alone in the dark
Waiting for you, and I wish
You didn't say you'd go with that guy…

The world between us not nearly so great a distance,
As I feel my existence from you;
I told you I would be your man and ask you…Oh! I spoke a lie.
My thoughts are cardboard, and words are just paper,
So I lost you over to that guy…

I speak paper words, I think cardboard thoughts
In confidence without any substance, and think myself a lie;
You only like smooth talkers, hanging cigarettes from lips of disdain
For stalkers lacking courage, welcoming friends without morals or misgivings;
And how can I compete with that guy?

…And I sit here again all alone in the dark,
Waiting for you to come so we won't be apart;
But for you love has learned what I still can't be taught:
I'm just another lonely guy with paper words and cardboard thoughts.

DEATH OF A MASOCHIST

He is the masochist. Drink to his health,
He won't have it for long.
Woe to the masochist. At heart he is weak,
But he's got to be strong.
You may ask a masochist:
Why hate yourself, your life's dark and dim.
No fun for a masochist:
He sees only hate, but it comes from within.

Oh, a man can't bear
The world on his shoulders!
You can punish yourself
For the sins of the world,
And your own,
'Till you're bloody and beaten and broken…

I met with the masochist:
So down on himself; what a sad way to go!
Poor, sad, angry masochist:
He's his worst foe, and he can't even know.
Too bad for the masochist:
His life was spent in self-punishment.
I'm sad for that masochist:
He couldn't forget his woes of resentment.

Oh, a man can't bear
The world on his shoulders!
You can punish yourself
For the sins of the world,
And your own,
'Till you're bloody and beaten and broken…

The masochist died today:
He couldn't find hope so he saw only ashes
Oh, why did you go away?
Now we mourn the death of a masochist.

NORMALCY NOW

I think this time,
I may have given up.
It's a struggle just to live my life today,
Without the ways I knew;
I'm going under,
And I can't save myself this time.
This new confusion,
—Or the old struggle—
Describes a perfect circle of despair,
And newness wearing thin;
A trapdoor opens beneath me in the stage of life:
It swallows me whole from the inside, again.
Just like days of old, I scream,
Pounding on the glass that only I can feel,
Until I bleed the words I long to see,
But speechless to be heard;
I shut up, and pretend I am okay:
No, not really.
Save myself now, steady breath;
Break from the still endless cycle.
I look around, and
The world screams confusion, too,
Assuring me
This is normalcy now.

BREAK THE SURFACE

This feeling is too much to handle,
I need to feel a breath of freedom from myself;
This inefficient life
Is too oppressive, I need to fight
And break free,
For I must find the answer
To kill the evil panic inside of me;
This lies residing
Somewhere in the catacombs of confusion;
Racked beneath my cross to bear,
The surface lies beyond me.
It is too far from my reach,
So now
Is eternal frustration the anthem of my downfall?
Angry torment flies undaunted, taunting me:
I am the oppressor,
Bear witness to my liberation!
As dying anger tries to pull me under in
One last gasp of misery,
Each heartbeat becomes strangled.
Die, tyrant mind!
This selfsame loss is inconsequential:
As the panic rots away,
I break the surface.

I DON'T SUFFER JUST TO MAKE A FASHION STATEMENT

I never noticed
So many people suffering
Only for attention,
Until I looked in the mirror
And realized
They were only faking their suffering.
I am not some trendy disorder;
I am the real deal.
Forever,
I am a square peg
Living in the round hole
Called life;
I cry out, because
My suffering is purely autistic.
A result of
Slow social perception,
I am misguided
By defects beyond my control;
You see a freak, where
I see normalcy.
The world around me
Is the only freak show apparent.
My ways
Do not always make sense,
Leaving vulnerable
Empty exposed wounds,
Bleeding from bullets
Shot out of your
Cruel laughter;
I am more alone than ever
On my own,
But feel free to misunderstand,
As I
Only act weird and stupid
For your
Ridiculous sense of amusement,
Not because
I am a human soul,

Born to be understanding
And soak up the misery
Of others
To cough up
Blood of indifference;
Please continue being amused by my ways,
Pay no attention
To the man
Behind the curtain of misery,
Or try to understand me
And see:
I don't suffer
Just to make a fashion statement.

TECHNOCRATIC ANARCHY

As the sun came up on this day,
I made a vow to kill technology
In each and every way;
I'm just a simple man.
I see no master plan.
Why can't I understand this way?

It's technocratic anarchy.
I'll break the system, and break free
From this maze of new technology;
This crazy plan will work,
Just wait and you will see.
So just remember the next time
When you see me:
I freed the world in technocratic anarchy.

If the day comes to cart me off;
I'll simply run past them and laugh at them,
And as they stare I'll scoff:
You thought that I would break.
That was your big mistake.
Go away before I crush you like a moth.

It's technocratic anarchy.
It's there for all of you to see,
Like chains that choked the life from me.
I broke the system,
And, in doing so, broke free
From this frustration
That I call technology;
And now there's only technocratic anarchy.

When I cease to live where I exist,
I'll stand up proudly on my Judgment Day,
They'll stare down from their list:
"This is our darkest day.
What do you have to say?"
I'll only smile, and raise my fist:

Oh, technocratic anarchy.

They could not kill my view of me.
I am no more a slave to technology;
I fought back, and destroyed
The things frustrating me;
Don't patronize, since
I don't care if you agree.
I won my war of technocratic anarchy.

SHALLOW MINDS

I am alone…
And I've known from the beginning
Of this dark, tortured soul's existence;
I am afraid…
And I feel there is no escaping
From the pain caused by my emptiness:
I want to be alive,
In love,
I want to feel that this life has meaning.
In this idiot's parade,
Faking lighthearted laughter,
There is no soul within this angry heart
Worthy of true love,
Only this walking cliché of purely dark light,
Aching to feel something
Apart from this rage,
Slowly burning me alive from this pit I dug
For emotions to die within
My sphere of
Claustrophobic difference;
Meanwhile,
I waste my words on deaf ears,
Consumed only by
Futile, shallow minds.

LAMENT FOR POINTLESSNESS

This effort,
It is a fatalistic flaw closing in for the kill
Of time well spent in vain;
Tick the years away,
The black widow to the death of me;
From stress, I am lost to time.
I linger within this dark realm,
Slowly pushing my worry uphill,
Only to crash down on me,
Like the futile efforts of every day
Closing in to crush me, and I bleed misery
From hard work;
It is lost to nothingness in the end.
So, again I cry,
Weeping from said futility,
Drinking sleeplessness,
Living as a dying soul for another day,
Drunk on labor lost
When gaining results
Breeds only lies;
I am brought back to my original woe.
There is no end, light has died.
And, lost in failure,
I lament for pointlessness.

AUTISTIC STATISTIC

The sadness you gave me
Has been seeping through my chest;
I feel it caress me,
As I start to get depressed;
And I often wonder how
I can still stand it now.
As I join the ranks of hopelessness:

I won't become an autistic statistic.
It will only make me be pessimistic.
Even through the static in your voice,
I can still see I don't have a choice.
I'm no victim of your twisted logistic:
I won't become your autistic statistic.

My pointless confusion
Builds the story of my life;
It seeks to destroy me,
As I drown in endless strife;
This is getting out of hand.
When will you understand?
I don't need this undeserving stress:

I won't become an autistic statistic.
Sorry, I'm not into being sadistic.
Even through the static in your voice,
I can still see I don't have a choice.
I'm no victim of your twisted logistic:
I won't become your autistic statistic.

I won't be pessimistic.
This lie is so sadistic.
Screw your so-called logistic:
I am not just an autistic statistic.

I won't become an autistic statistic.
I don't care if my words make you ballistic.
Even through the static in your voice,
I'm okay, since I made my own choice.
I'm no victim of your twisted logistic:
I was never your autistic statistic.

THROUGH THIS GLASS PRISM OF AGGRAVATION

I am a walking slice of nothing
Built on broken dreams;
I smile, but only wearing this mask
Of false happiness:
I wear it to show the world
I can't be defeated.
Every day, the illusion breaks a little,
Forming cracks within
This broken machine called effort;
Every day, I die within myself,
And as I watch, the world passes by
Free from frustration;
I consume it all, chasing light,
Emitting only darkness,
Everyone else receives my efforts but me.
I am the one the parasite enjoys
As I cry alone, and
I expend my energy on pointlessness.
Watching the world endlessly, I bleed envy,
Jealously watching the lives of the masses:
Easy friendships, time to kill,
Success is with panic not included.
This is the intangible life I long to lead, and
I watch vaguely, through this glass prism of aggravation.

BLOCKADE

There lies in words without cares
Your hopes and the world you know;
Cold words and cold stares,
Your thoughts you dare not show.
No one will understand,
When they are blinded from truth…

Kiss your entire dreams goodbye,
No one here will see you cry,
When in between you
There's the silence of a barrier.
The walls close in around you;
You walk into your own stockade,
And face the mess that you have made;
You are now the barrier.
You're alone behind your own blockade…

Lies separate the anguish
Inside your bothered mind;
Words are in fragments of English,
Is truth so hard to find?
No one will understand
When they are blinded from truth…

Kiss your entire dreams goodbye,
No one here will see you cry,
When in between you
There's the silence of a barrier.
The walls close in around you;
You walk into your own stockade,
And face the mess that you have made;
You are now the barrier.
You're alone behind your own blockade…

I tell myself for once, for all:
"Tear down this wall!"
But I am no longer listening.
Trapped within my own stockade,
The walls crash down, thundering,
And I can see the mess I've made,
Trapped behind my own blockade…

…No one will understand,
When they are blinded from truth:
We are our own blockade.

OVERREACTION

Bleeding skies,
The world ablaze ten times over,
Raging, ranting inarticulately,
Simple words are a red flag
For this tormented soul.
It must seem psychotic,
—Like a real cause for concern—
But this is what I see.
Struck by sudden disorderliness,
I panic,
Screaming in tongues
Without noticing
The frightened stares of everyone;
I soon find the root of my pointless strife.
Condemning myself to my own
Submissive shame,
I retreat to the dark, where I
Cower in my lonely corner.
Cursing myself,
A foolish panicking victim I am.
Never in control,
A lone romancer
To the mistress of pain,
I ask God why this must be.
In the end,
Only He could deliver me
From my inward Hell,
But I always see him turned away,
Maddeningly ignoring me;
For I know this:
I am my own dictation
Of my totalitarian mental state of panic,
Bowing down
To the next irrational fear;
Forever submissive,
I wait to prove myself insane again,
In a redundant state
Of crazed
Overreaction.

ALL THAT I HEAR

This is the sound of struggle,
This is the sound of pain.
This is the same unchanging sound
Over and over again;

This is the sound of anger,
This is the sound of strife.
This is the sound of sharpened words,
Cutting through me like a knife;

This is the sound of crying,
This is the sound of war.
This is the sound of pointless stress
Leaving me begging for more;

This is the sound of screaming,
This is the sound of rage.
This is the sound of hands on bars,
My hands, inside of this cage;

This is the sound of darkness,
This is the sound of sleep.
This is the sound that I can't have
While I curl up and I weep;

This is the sound of failure,
This is the sound that I fear.
This is the sound of each new day,
But now, it is all that I hear.

WRATH OF A NOT-GOD

High and mighty,
You sit on your throne,
Looking down on me,
A mere mortal;
I bow to your all-knowing greatness.
It is all in your head.
Behind your computer screen,
You have just as much courage as the man
You proclaim yourself
To be above;
But no trumpets herald your praises,
No angels exalt your name on high.
A false idol
Carved in imitation stone,
You serve to judge
Your fellow man,
The object of your scorn;
You are insignificant, like us.
I distrust your so-called superiority,
Used only for the sake of
Putting me down
Into my place of shame
You built inside your own mind.
My talents are worth less than dirt to you;
You dislike the idea that
Other people can be well-liked.
To you,
This concept is sinful;
It is worthy of your condemnation.
So, you build a wall of followers,
A fellowship of fools,
Worshipping
In their parish of idiocy;
It is a mass Mecca of moronic proportions.
"All Hail the Jesus of the Dumb!
Grace His Self-Serving Name!"
What a laugh.
You don't impress me, in fact,
You disgust me.

You exist
Only to deliver me to your promised land
Of disgrace;
But I reject it all,
Too proud to waste my time
Worrying about
The wrath of a Not-God.

AD NAUSEUM (UNTIL WE HAVE SEEN ENOUGH)

My friends, I know you are skeptical,
But, hear me out.
We are on a path to our own destruction.
Our leaders deny the truth;
Those we trust have failed.
Violence and chaos
Rain from the hearts of the unjust;
We are the children of our fathers.
Selfsame rebels of the past,
They work to prevent our eventual downfall.
Pass the burden on,
Sour wine of a broken covenant;
We are just pawns in this game
Without a winner;
Figures of the past, rise up,
Condemn the failures of the reforms
We seek.
Today, we are the future.
Tomorrow, we will be history.
Fight for this world now,
It is not too late for us.
Let the song of hope
Be heard among this broken generation:
A new-age fight song
Will guide the masses;
Clear these black clouds
From our souls,
Touch the face of purity.
We were all once trapped
In our own cage of self-doubt,
Bloody still from yesterday's struggle;
Born again to save ourselves,
We cry for our demise.
Lost along the way,
We have seen this all before.
Stains on the conscience of eternity,
We disgrace ourselves;
We are the cause of this demon

Called Humanity;
Sinners in the worst way,
Blame each other for your own iniquities:
You'll only die faster.
Mark the seven deadly sins:
These are the devils we follow.
Mark the graves lost for blood and empire,
No one can save you from
This curse we share.
Decimate our mortal shrines,
We shall rebuild our shame.
So it goes, on into ad nauseum,
Until we have seen enough.

PUT UP AND SHUT UP

Walk along your street
Of imagined greatness;
Nobody walks there but you.
You look down upon me
Like something worthless;
I've become dirt on your shoe.
I just give you a smirk,
'Cause the insults don't work,
And you're only a jerk in the end.
Now, listen to the message I send:

I might seem odd,
But that won't make you God,
Just dirt on the face of the human race;
Put up and shut up is all I ask,
Don't fake perfection behind your mask.
The world will give you up,
So put up and shut up.

Stare down on the world
Like we're all beneath you;
Everyone drowns in their shame.
No chance to escape,
No way we can break through;
Everything still stays the same.
You might think that you're tough,
But now I've had enough,
You are all the wrong stuff in the end.
Now, listen to the message I send:

I might seem odd,
But that won't make you God,
Just dirt on the face of the human race;
Put up and shut up is all I ask,
Don't fake perfection behind your mask.
The world will give you up,
So put up and shut up.

I know I made your bubble burst,
But my dignity always comes first.

And I don't care, but that's okay:
I would have ignored you anyway.

I might seem odd,
But that won't make you God,
Just dirt on the face of the human race;
Put up and shut up is all I ask,
Don't fake perfection behind your mask.
The world will give you up,
So put up and shut up.

LANCE BASS IS GAY (A Spoof on Various Rich and Famous People, 2007)

I must be the only person who can see that
Every big story involves a big star.
Whitney got arrested for doing the drugs,
And Paris got a DUI while driving her car.
But though the media seems to care,
We've all seen stars in their underwear.

Lindsey got a boob job,
Justin won a Grammy.
The whole world's in love
With the guy who said, "WHAMMY!"
Whoopi lost weight,
Hillary got dumped.
Michael likes little boys,
Rosie got Trump-ed.
Does this news really matter anyway?
Now the boy-bands suck,
Since Lance Bass is gay.

Everyone's so self-obsessed they don't care
About all the poor people dying in Darfur;
Rap artists are gods, and pop music rules.
Suddenly new talent becomes one big blur.
But it's only been twelve years of strife
Since O. J. killed his wife!

Catholic priests are perverts,
Kramer is a racist.
SNL and Family Guy say
Disney was a fascist.
Elvis lives in legend,
But Diana's still dead.
And everyone is laughing
At what Dane Cook said.
Does this news really matter anyway?
Now boy-bands suck,
Since Lance Bass is gay.

You might be respected,
But there is just one glitch:
You can't be popular
If you're ugly or not rich;
And this may all seem crazy,
But this is what I see,
As sure as South Park
Finds new ways to kill Kenny!

Does this news really matter anyway?
Now the boy-bands suck,
Since Lance Bass is gay.
It's the truth, and it won't go away.
Why do people care if Lance Bass is gay?

WORST-CASE SCENARIO

This afternoon I had another meltdown,
A level-four panic attack,
Another four-alarm red-letter day;
It seemed like everything was going so well, so what?
I got kicked in the face,
Slapped down by "the Man" and put in my place again.
There's nothing I can do except complain;
As God as my witness, I'm at my wit's end.
I'm lost in a fog of confusion,
Trapped in a cage of frustration;
I hate this technology, and I have no apology.
These things don't work to any end,
But it feeds the stressful life I lead.
I rant long past the point of words failing,
Digging my own grave through inadequacy,
Bathing in the darkness of my beautiful heart attack
This world intended for me to suffer.
God would not place a burden too heavy
For good and decent people to handle;
Well, only the good die young.
Unless they fight to live this lie, they too shall fall into oblivion.
So welcome to my lifelong struggle,
A battle for the right to my own contentment,
It's scattered on the rocks of my worst-case scenario.

I'M RIGHT

I'm wrong when I'm happy,
I'm wrong when I glare.
I'm wrong when I'm stupid,
I'm wrong when I care.

I'm wrong when I'm losing,
I'm wrong when I win.
I'm wrong when I'm decent,
I'm wrong when I sin.

I'm wrong when I'm failing,
I'm wrong when I try.
I'm wrong when I'm cheerful,
I'm wrong when I cry.

I'm wrong when I'm clueless,
I'm wrong when I know.
I'm wrong when I'm staying,
I'm wrong when I go.

I'm wrong when I'm silent,
I'm wrong when I speak.
I'm wrong when I'm hiding,
I'm wrong when I seek.

I'm wrong when I'm guessing
I'm wrong, but not quite:
I'm wrong for believing
I'm wrong…since I'm right.

SUPERFICIAL

All of you,
Look at this judgment focused upon me
For the sake of the mass ego,
Wanting to burn me at the stake
Like the gods you believe yourselves to be;
I am worthy of this indignation in your eyes,
But only in your eyes,
The eyes that cut like poison razorblades
Though the gates of my soul;
This is not the way it should be.
I am not the fool you see.
This world denies my worth,
As though I'm not meant for this world;
Like the vermin underneath your feet,
You squash
My hopes and dreams beneath your odious words,
Foul with the venom of
Superiority you see within yourself,
Only falsely seen through the eyes of ignorance;
Can't you see the flaws of your beliefs?
You are a puppet, and Society is your master;
You are not the boss of me,
When you cannot see
Your judgment is nothing short of superficial.

ME AND THE PAVEMENT

Feet pounding the pavement, head bobbing,
The ground lies flat ahead of me;
My troubles lie in the rearview.
This is my escape, and the world is my prison.
Empty minds,
Thinking empty closed-minded thoughts:
This is the misery of me,
And the lies slice my throat with ignorance;
It's me against the world again, but I am not outnumbered.
On the road,
Where my sneakers pound out my own beat
And the voices fade away,
I run away from the madness,
The laughter and shame of the fools;
In their black-and-white checkerboard world, they rule.
Society holds no power here where I run,
Free from depression;
I know that I'll be just fine in the end.
I'm running for myself,
And I don't need your approval or your authority.
No more pretending,
Since I'm running away from you and your lies;
I feel okay, when
It's just me and the pavement.

SHADOW ALIBI

Bleed the river dry
With thoughts of imperfection,
The curse of you, the plight of me;
My mind runs in circles,
—Tailspin from the within—
As I starve my better judgment
To feed the beast of unjust blame,
I lie in wait for my release
From the guillotine of condescension;
Take what is yours, but leave me this hollow self
In retribution for my unmarked sins,
Lost from truth I am;
Underscored by the innocence,
It smells like a rose,
Rots more like the fungus of the earth.
Cry for me,
I bathe in your crocodile tears
Shed by the victory always at my expense,
Live for the good of the greater lie.
Doomed by your indignation,
The shame lives in vain;
When the world comes undone for you,
Naked at the threshold of pretension,
Lying humbled at the sight of your shadow alibi.

IN THESE DELUDED EYES

Who am I to blame
When all I can see
Is the same broken path paved in frustration?
Dark blinded mind
Like a bat in the daytime,
I stumble along in my own lost light.

In these deluded eyes, all I see is darkness.
In these deluded eyes, all I am is wrong.

This is the same story
From a different book
Written by the great unknown inept
Oppressing us all;
We deserve something more.
But fate will not be denied our downfall.
.

In these deluded eyes, all I see is failure.
In these deluded eyes, all I know is wrong.

So save for the silence of forsaken apathy,
I am bound by the chains of my human flaws.
The shame is mine; for my unfounded guilt resides
Without the hope of compromise in these deluded eyes.

BRUTAL LEGACY

This is what you've become,
Full circle to again begin;
And to violence still succumb,
You advocate your hate and sin.

So this is how you live your life,
Live to hate, hate to love.
This is why you live to die,
Die to cause the whole world pain,
Pain you love to spread to us;
We're the ones to bear the cross,
A cross you want the world to see,
And that's your brutal legacy.

Blame the world for your hurt,
The hurt you built for your demise;
Bathe within the blood you spurt,
A blank expression's your disguise.

So this is how you live your life,
Live to hate, hate to love.
This is why you live to die,
Die to cause the whole world pain,
Pain you love to spread to us;
We're the ones to bear the cross,
A cross you want the world to see,
And that's your brutal legacy.

The hopes and dreams are gone,
For us, and crucify yourself.
Still you scorn the hopeful dawn,
And bask within your hateful wealth.

And so this is your life you chose,
Your life you lived for us to see;
So now you lie in death's repose,
And so fulfilled your prophecy;
You made your brutal legacy.

ALL IS DONE

Another chance wasted, defeat newly tasted,
The same story from a sharpened view,
Clamping down to start anew;
Why are we wasting our time, wasting away?
Get up and seize the day!
Give your life a whole new rhyme.
It doesn't help to feel so down, perk up!
Wring a smile from that frown, get up!
Stand tall, and stand your ground.
Tomorrow comes another chance,
Wait and yours will come around
Without a second glance;
Seasons change, within range
Of everything you'll ever need;
Don't concede
That life will change too late for you:
It's true,
The going's tough when you're behind,
But you won't mind.
On top of the world, with flags unfurled,
A golden destiny far from the madness,
No more wracked in sadness;
You finally won the war you begun,
Now rest; all is done.

WEB OF LIES

I've tried to ignore it,
But I just can't endure it;
Lying through your teeth,
Insecurity beneath
All the yawning tales you've told.

It's hard to accept you,
When I still can't tell what's true;
Try to put me down,
But you still look like a clown,
And it's starting to get old.

The things that you've told me
All seem like pure baloney;
Try to play the friend,
So my trust can still defend
How you put me in my place.

The world seems much smaller.
Does it make you feel taller?
Looking down on me,
So that you won't have to see
Lies are written on your face.

I don't see the reason
To put up with your treason;
Taking credit for
All I ever did and more,
Building castles in the skies.

It's time that I spoke up,
So maybe you will shut up;
I see what you are,
So you can't crawl very far
In your tangled web of lies.

SOMEONE I'M NOT

I can be witty,
And I can be charming;
I'll bring you laughter
With smiles disarming;
I'll be perfection
As you like to see;
And anything else,
But I'll still just be me.

I can be stupid,
But not be a fool;
I'll show you crazy
And prove that it's cool;
I'll sing you songs
Where you'll get up and dance;
But give up myself–
No, I won't take a chance!

I can be truthful,
And bring you to tears;
I'll give you memories
To last through the years;
I'll be a lover,
A brother, a friend;
But true sense of self–
That's the thing I'll defend.

I can be selfless,
And give you my all;
I'll be your servant
That heeds to your call;
I'll live devoted
'Till death when I rot;
But won't do a thing,
If I'm someone I'm not.

…'Cause I just don't care
To be someone I'm not.

MILE IN MY SHOES

There's too much apathy in here,
And too much anger fed by fear;
Where's the love?
Too much blood that we have shed,
And too much hatred we have fed;
Look above:
There we see the angels crying,
As our hearts and bodies dying
Frame the ground
In an epithet of sadness,
Fueled by great and tragic madness;
Look around.
This will more than surely pass,
As words we said both cruel and crass
Fade away;
Like shadows on the moonlit stair,
Or demons that have wandered there
Not to stay.
Look upon your tortured mind,
And more than not you'll often find
Life's not bad.
The human race will victimize,
And vilify and demonize
As it had;
But actions of a loving heart
Can make a most endearing art;
Wait and see.
The good will get what they deserve
And so the goodwill that they serve
Comes to be,
At least as far as I've been told
By all the wishes that I've sold
To the well,
In hopes that you will learn to feel
The good side of the Karma wheel;
Time will tell.
So hark to heed the words I say,
And as you run to seize the day,
You can't lose.
Now stand up tall and proud and smile,
Since you deserve it for this mile
In my shoes.

FOUND MY WAY

Where's the way out of all this stress?
This all-consuming madness—
It's leading me astray,
When all I want to do is get away;
Disorganization—
All it's given me is mental constipation.
But now I'm through,
Since all you do
Has given me reasons to feel blue:

I'm writing this obligatory
Poem about feeling happy,
For reasons that I cannot say;
I need a happy ending to this story,
And I won't say I'm sorry.
I won't let life rain on my day;
I found my way.

This world just feeds the lives we lead,
And cuts the lies that we bleed;
I'm falling to the floor,
Still getting up and coming back for more.
Living my frustration,
All I'm receiving is endless consternation.
So now I'm through,
Since all you do
Has given me reasons to feel blue:

I'm writing this obligatory
Poem about feeling happy,
For reasons that I cannot say;
I need a happy ending to this story,
And I won't say I'm sorry.
I won't let life rain on my day;
I found my way.

I can't take this anymore,
I'm walking out that door
If I cannot be free;
The list goes on and on,

But when you see I'm gone
You'll know it's not for me…

So here's my obligatory
Poem about feeling happy,
And I've said all that I can say.
I found a happy ending to this story,
I never said that I was sorry.
This life will not rain on my day,
I found my way.

ICONIC INCONSIDERATION

This is a sound-off
For the kids of today:
The generation that believes
They come first.
It's all about them,
Who cares about what I want,
Isn't that right?
That's the plan
For the breakdown
Of a new American century;
Built to fuel apathy
Among the quiet,
Considerate few,
So we can be hurt.
Everything is okay
As long as we smile;
If I complain,
That makes me the bad guy.
If you are wrong,
Congratulations.
You must be normal
By today's standards;
Not like me:
What a deluded weirdo
I am
To dream of decency
For all,
And not just your obnoxious chosen ones;
Fuel the flames
Of your fires ignited
By ignorance,
As you hide behind your banners:
Racist,
Uptight cracker,
Freak, retard, zealot—UGH!
You'll say anything to claim that
You're right.
But I will not be broken.
The time has come
To speak up,

Speak out,
Stand up,
Stand out,
And be heard.
For though I am a man,
My words form a mountain
Of truth,
Crushing your right
To oppress me,
With your new-age
Iconic inconsideration.

ALL YOU'LL EVER GET

If my apathy upsets you,
And my jokes can make you smile,
Well, you know my inner torment?
It's completely worth the while.

If my actions work to scare you,
And befuddle you with rhyme,
Then you might not understand me,
So you're just not worth my time.

If my honest ways corrupt you,
And my genius strikes you dumb,
Then we're both on different wavelengths;
I move to a different drum.

If you feel your life is screwy,
And each day is but a curse,
Then it might seem quite surprising
When I tell you I've had worse.

If you haven't read this poem,
Then you'll still be clueless yet;
I have told you all about me,
And that's all you'll ever get.

UNDER TYRANNY OF CONSCIENCE

If I had wings,
I would fly away from here;
Off to a place where
I am free,
A place just for me:
Where the stress of the world
Slides off my back;
Off into oblivion it falls.
No one can hurt me
In my safe place
Like I hurt myself, when
Caring too much is my dagger.
Why can't I escape?
The cage expands
But the bars remain intact,
Just the way it's always been;
I'm playing the same old character,
In a different story
By a new author,
But the situations remain the same.
The repetition becomes a blur,
A black, blurry void
Of darkness;
This darkness I must escape.
The light is there,
Always dancing away
At my touch,
A touch from different hands;
These are the hands
Of my inconvenient truth;
This truth is my blessing:
A double-edged sword
Also tainted with curses,
Working from within for my demise;
This demise I deny myself.
I protest against it.
My limitations shall not overtake me,
Like I overtook myself

In an effort to be something better,
Better than I am;
I am not my limitations,
My limitations are not my master.
Knowing this truth fuels me forward,
Beyond the limits of myself,
My worst enemy;
The one I always fight;
I am he, under tyranny of conscience.

THE DAY THE LIGHT WENT AWAY

When decency died, nobody had cried
For good we washed away on that sad day;
We blackened our hearts, and now everyone starts
To wither and fall; we felt nothing at all
That day our decency died.

When honesty burned, the world had still turned
As beauty turned to ash mired in trash;
We all turned our cheek, so the truth could not speak
For all that we were; begging fate to differ
That day our honesty burned.

When kindness was killed, the blood had been spilled
By idols we had made; no one dismayed.
We no longer cared, for the sadness we shared
Of better days gone; in this gray ashen dawn
We wept for kindness we killed.

When light went away, not much did we say
But sat, gave up, and wept. Fitful we slept;
We felt in our mind, for the truth left behind
We lost long ago; but we honestly know
The day the light went away.

ELEGANCE OF CONTINUOUS BEWILDERMENT

Is there anyone listening in this world?
Do they know this fog where I wander?
Condemned by my weaknesses,
Disappointment is my elixir.
Welcome, words in broken thought,
Enter my mind and take my truth away.
Now I am lost, running in circles,
Circling bewilderment around me;
This is the elegance in the mind of the warped.
I am the enigma without logic!
Bending reality,
I do this through misinterpretation.
An eye of a needle or the tears of a clown,
What does it matter in this false perception?
Lies abound while truth dwindles;
Ineptness pulls this soul asunder.
Still, I will not be perplexed.
As my unreachable goals goad me,
I seek to strive against the world.
Prove this beauty from within,
Teach me the ways of confusion to abate the tide!
Find the strength in my will of stone,
To preserve that which makes no sense at all:
Long live the elegance of continuous bewilderment.

MY BIOGRAPHY, AS TOLD THROUGH A POEM IN ONLY TEN LINES

Jim—
Helpful, honest, happy;
—Relative of all people who desire freedom from oppression, depression, and temptation,
Lover of Christ, fine art, and superheroes;
I am one who feels confused, clarified, and verified all at once;
I am one who fears eternal damnation, being ignored, and jellyfish;
I am one who needs hugs, praise, and sometimes more explanation;
I am one who would like to see Mount Rushmore, future times, and happiness among all creatures of the earth;
Resident of anywhere I am needed,
—Madonna

ALL THESE THINGS REMAIN THE SAME

Tell my friends my head exploded,
Confidence in life eroded,
Wonder why my dreams imploded;
As I watch, the world rolls by.

Used to love but love's a lie,
Must be crazy if I try,
Slowly all my hopes just die;
As I sit, I rot in shame.

Trapped within my lust's desire,
Up to my neck in this mire,
Leading me into the fire;
Naked, soaked in sweat I cry.

Tortured by my conscious mind,
Searching for what I won't find,
Wanting what I left behind;
Losing, I won't play this game.

Doing ill through good intention,
Just enough to breed dissension,
In the light of past invention;
Truth evades my naked eye.

Let this be your lesson learned,
Speaking out will leave you burned,
Nothing left that you have earned;
All these things remain the same.

OH, AWKWARDNESS
THE BEAUTIFUL
(To the tune of "America the Beautiful")

Oh, retailers of shirts and pants, please hear my desperate plea:
Whenever I go shop for clothes, there's nothing that fits me!
Oh, clothing stores, oh, clothing stores,
Please spare my dignity!
Make clothing that will fit my shape, and end my misery!

Oh, booger from within my nose, so gooey, gross and green:
My sneezing stuck it on my chin, and made me cause a scene!
Oh, nasal gunk, oh, nasal gunk,
Revolting is your sheen!
And though I wash, and wash again, my chin shall not get clean!

Oh, pimple throbbing on my face, so pus-filled, large and white:
Each time the ladies see you there, they run away in fright!
Oh, greasy skin, oh, greasy skin,
Remove me of this plight!
For maybe if it clears in time, I'll have a date tonight!

CAN'T WRITE A POEM, SO I'LL WRITE A BOOK

I can't write a poem,
My head is too clogged;
My nose is too stuffy,
My eyes are all fogged.

I can't write a poem,
There's too much to do;
There's places to be, and
I might have the flu.

I can't write a poem,
My brain is on hold;
My chair is too warm, and
My desk is too cold.

I can't write a poem,
I'm simply too tired;
I'm not too creative,
I'm just not inspired.

I can't write a poem,
It's just too much work;
It's too hard to read, and
It's made me berserk.

I can't write a poem,
So don't even look;
I might never finish,
So I'll write a book.

SNAPSHOT FROM PRIOR TO COLLEGE

Two young men standing together as friends
In the photo near my television
Smile at me as I smile at them;
Those men are a friend and me in younger days.
A guitar case rests by the window,
The window is part of the porch at the front of my beach house.
Keith, as my friend is called,
Still has that guitar and case,
And I still have the beach house, window intact.
It was not that long ago,
But long enough that neither of us had grown goatees yet,
And I was still without my hat.
I was just out of high school;
−Keith was held back in eighth grade, so he still had another year−
I looked forward to tomorrow.
Well, tomorrow has come, after much ado.
Me, Keith, and my Aunt Chris (the one holding the camera);
All of us are still here, and slightly older.
But we two friends have goatees,
And my aunt has had a knee replaced,
The guitar a few strings replaced.
But we're still the same people in the snapshot from prior to college.

SICK

I'm so sick of feeling so bad.
I'm so sick of looking so fat.
I'm so sick of not being trusted.
I'm so sick of the fights with you.
I'm so sick of my clothes feeling tight.
I'm so sick of my reflection depressing me.
I'm so sick of joking to hide my pain.
I'm so sick of living a lie I won't see.
I'm so sick of hiding when I overeat.
I'm so sick of the "fat talk" from everyone.
I'm so sick of dreading visits to the doctor.
I'm so sick of being the fat friend.
I'm so sick of hurtful names that are true.
I'm so sick of my narrow, unhealthy food preferences.
I'm so sick of not being one of the hot guys.
I'm so sick of avoiding the bathroom scale.
I'm so sick of living in denial.
I'm so sick of not having self-control.
I'm so sick of using my Asperger Syndrome as a crutch.
I'm so sick of envying my friends' bodies.
I'm so sick of knowing that I ate too much.
I'm so sick of bending down to see my genitals.
I'm so sick of good pants that no longer fit.
I'm so sick of my persistent unwillingness to listen to you.
I'm so sick of hating healthy people.
I'm so sick of blaming you for my weakness.
I'm so sick of always being out of breath.
I'm so sick of being such a glutton.
I'm so sick of having to make excuses.
I'm so sick of giving in to my cravings.
I'm so sick of causing you so much worry.
I'm so sick of my weight oppressing me.
I'm just so sick of feeling so sick.

FREEDOM OF SELF

Silence the thoughts,
The emptiness inside;
Overwhelming
Loss of direction;
Talking heads telling me:
"Pick a side!
There's no room for indifference!"
Faith is lost,
Bleeding out, running down,
Leaving me alone;
I'm more alone than I've ever been.
I need some space
Left to feel safe,
So there's nothing for you to take away.
I used to see the light,
Only replaced with darkness,
Mocking my life
With sad happy lies;
When will it stop?
Then I can be like you want me to be.
Not like this, like I want to be;
Free to worship,
Free to be indifferent:
At last, I'll have freedom of self.

HERE WE GO AGAIN

Watch the news as the day dies;
Another masquerade of misery,
Misfortune, bad news, and debate all coated in lies:
They say that they are just like me.

Read the paper with your tea;
An hour lost on another sad thing,
As the ringmaster beckons the peanut gallery:
"Draw your eyes to the center ring!"

Hear ye, hear ye not.
Hear me, hear them not.
There's no such thing as truth,
There's no such time as youth.
We're just a cog in the machine,
We're just a clog in the latrine.
Hear us, hear us not.
Read the news that we can't use,
Hear it, hear it not.
All you hear is just a ruse.

Here I go again, there you go again.
There it goes again, here we go again.

THE ALIEN

I am the alien:
Wrapped in silent sadness,
Wandering through your world,
Longing for belonging;
This world is not my home.
Though these people look like me,
I am not like them.
I know I am different,
I have known this fact all my life.
The wise ones tell me the reasons,
But what do they know?
They have not lived my internal separation,
They only allowed it.
Lost in the onslaught of stimuli,
I miss your cues;
These tell me how to blend in.
But the others sense my lacking sameness,
And reject me;
They favor their own kind.
Defeated, I return to the familiar scrutiny
Of your efforts to unlock my mystery;
You cannot change me.
Only can you teach me your ways,
And I shall hope to learn.
My destiny lies in the hands of this world.
Our world has many of you,
Though it has few of me.
This is the reality of my existence:
I remain continually unsure.
This is not new for me;
According to what I am told,
I struggle with many things.
Yet for you,
These things come easy.
I often wish I could change this fact.
Tell me honestly:
If I am of this world,
Why do I feel so foreign?
You don't have to answer me.
I doubt you can truly answer me.
But say something!

Say kind words at least, and
Show me I belong.
It would be nice, if only for a while.
At the end of the day, still,
I am the alien.

STRANGE

Accommodation unreturned,
Consideration never learned;
Live to die another day,
Be a tool another way.
Fight the tide and stoke the fire,
More blood fed to this vampire.
And all these things will never change,
If speaking out makes one look strange.

It never falters, never fails,
Watching as the truth derails;
Saying things you never mean,
Ignorance is on the scene.
Burning lives and breaking minds,
Hiding in your iron binds;
And finding hope is out of range,
When speaking out makes one look strange.

Hatred thrives with kindness spared,
Things would change if someone cared.
Worlds apart it's all the same;
Losing in the corporate game
Makes it hard for me to thrive,
Still defeated, still alive;
And all the while you still arrange
So speaking out makes me look strange.

(IN THE WAKE OF) FAILURE'S DEMISE

Once again frustration consumes me,
Tearing me apart
To stand naked and ashamed
Like I have done many times before;
Does it amuse you, cruel fate?
Do you like to watch me suffer?
Of course you do.
I resented this hand you dealt.
Powerless and bound
At the sound of your brutal laughter,
You cut me down again
To die a little more inside;
You just couldn't kill me enough,
Could you?
Involuntarily I bleed for you,
But I refuse to fall.
Staggering toward the sound of your jeers
Now with my hands around your throat,
It's your turn to submit
To the destiny of my victory,
As I watch you fall away;
Another demon is vanquished,
Never will it darken my soul again.
Washing my hands clean,
I stand strong and unburdened,
Raising my fist toward the heavens above;
I won't be broken again.
Left to stand alone as I am,
I stand before you now:
Bold and brave, proud and powerful,
Again
I am restored to my rightful place of honor.
I wear the blood of my inner apocalypse
As a badge of my epic odyssey,
Known only to me,
But still I stand victorious;
In the light of glory,
I shine in the wake of failure's demise.

AWAY FROM YOU

In mindless compliance
I silence my questions,
And trapped in complacence
I mute my dissensions;
How far have I come when I have gone numb?
Well, you might be appeased but I'll never be pleased.
Honey, this is the end, my friend.
It's clear you don't care
Whenever I dare
To assert how I feel,
With intent to reveal
I'm thinking of leaving, since you're so deceiving.
My words leave no sound, because you're not around.
Honey, this will not work, you jerk.
I speak and you listen,
But you won't be open,
So now I'm revolting
Against your insulting;
It's time I spoke out, so I won't be shut out
From the lies you promote and the hopes that you smote;
Honey, that's what you do, you shrew.
Now there's nothing left to do
Except clean the blood you drew,
So, I'll get away from you.

THIS POEM I JUST WROTE

If only I had more time,
I would have gone to bed earlier,
And woken up earlier, too;
I'd have eaten a bagel—
No, a croissant, perhaps,
And then had time to brush my teeth,
Maybe I'd have even taken a shower,
Still getting to my morning class on time;
It's all because of my writer's block
That kept me on the internet,
So I would procrastinate with another assignment,
Ultimately a-snooze at the crack of dawn,
Awaking not much later;
Oh, if only I had planned better!
I might have written that poem
Instead of tapping my pen aimlessly,
Drawing a continuous blank:
I might have written my masterpiece.
But…it wasn't meant to be.
So, please accept this blank piece of paper
As a peace offering
And let me go back to sleep,
Where I can dream of writing better poetry than
This poem I just wrote.

A TRIBUTE TO ANONYMOUS

Here's to that great writer,
Poet, storyteller,
And vast collector of anecdotes:
Here's to Anonymous, that prolific creator
Unknown by many writers and readers,
But still indigenous to many cultures;
Here's to the unknown author,
That constantly striving hard worker,
Never getting recognition
But still creating all the while,
Possibly only for their own reasons;
Here's to the longest living creative thinker
Ever to grace this earth
Longer than all the towering literary giants:
Giants named Shakespeare, Poe, Irving,
Dickens, Dickenson, and Blake–
–All were amateurs, in comparison
To that great unsung champion of poets;
Here's to the long-lived literary legend
Of many cultures and many times,
All intertwined into one,
With a vast collection
Of literary works more varied
And voluminous than you can ever imagine,
But far less celebrated than necessary,
As none were ever
More deserving of accolades;
Today we pay our just respects,
Tipping our hats in gratitude
And remembrance
To the hero that expanded our minds
And our libraries:
For that, all we can do is
Stand and give our thanks
In a tribute to Anonymous.

BIO POEM THE SECOND

Jim—
Cheerful, thoughtful, philosophically obtuse;
Relative of dreamers, the disabled, and my parents, of course!
Lover of life, good humor, and kind people;
I am one who feels hungry for knowledge, thirsty for faith, and indigestion at the current state of the world;
I am one who fears stereotyping, disorganization, and getting accused of the wrong crime;
I am one who needs love, laughter, and more time if needed;
I am one who would like to see a more lively, vibrant, and enthusiastic music scene;
Resident of the universe,
—Madonna.

HUMOR IS MY HEROIN

Humor is my heroin,
Life is my cocaine.
Philosophy became my weed,
My hope promotes my pain.

Humor is my heroin,
Love keeps me insane.
Thinking is my drug of choice,
My faith lets in the rain.

Humor is my heroin,
Friendship's my addiction.
Truth is my oppressor,
Laughter is my affliction.

Humor is my heroin,
Caring is my blight.
Drawing is my cigarette,
And writing is my light.

If humor is your heroin,
And peace a source of fright;
Come meet me in my misery,
So we'll have fun tonight!

INGREDIENTS FOR A GOOD, GORY, GENERIC HORROR MOVIE ABOUT A PSYCHOTIC SLASHER

Gather together a group of friends:
Two of whom will have sex,
One of whom is a funny guy,
One of whom is brooding and mysterious,
One of whom is a cautious girl,
One nice guy to be her boyfriend,
And the last one must be a stoner.
Put them all in a secluded area.
This can be a campground,
A house owned by someone's parents,
Or it can be an abandoned vacation spot.
Next, make sure they can't leave.
Once the victims—oops! travelers—are secure,
Just add in the killer for deadly fun.
Make sure our psycho is wearing a mask.
The mask can be a gas mask,
Maybe a hockey mask,
Or it can be a Halloween mask;
That way, he will look more threatening.
Give him a weapon for his killing spree;
Something with a sharp blade,
Like a butcher knife, a machete, a pickaxe,
Or a hook for a hand;
This is better to make for bloodier deaths.
Once our killer is fully equipped,
Separate each of the naïve, young innocents,
So nobody can hear or rescue them.
Do these next steps in the following order:
Kill the funny guy early on in the movie.
Later, kill the couple having sex.
Killing the stoner is not mandatory, as
No one else will believe him anyway.
Next, allow for the cautious one to go looking for her missing friends,
And find their mutilated, bloodied bodies.
After she finds the bodies,
It is natural for her to be alarmed,
And even falsely think the brooding mystery guy is the killer—

–Until the real killer kills him.
The next few minutes will be spent
Running in terror from our masked psychopath.
Screaming for help is optional,
But, it's greatly encouraged.
By now, there will be the killer, the victim,
…And seemingly no way to escape alive.
Bring the horror flick to a close by
Adding in a twist, that ends the killer's life.
You may use fire, guns, or activate traps.
For extra fun, have the cautious girl's boyfriend stab the killer in the back.
Feel free to film crappy sequels.

THE GOOD LORD STILL LOVES THEE

You've searched for perfection
That you'll never find,
And you've stared at the world
'Till you've all but gone blind,
And you'll just keep on looking
'Till you've lost your mind;
But don't worry, my friend,
You'll find truth in the end:
For the Good Lord still loves thee.

You've known many secrets
That no one should know,
And you've gone all the places
That no one should go,
And you live by the sword
So you reap what you sew;
But don't worry, my friend,
You'll find peace in the end:
For the Good Lord still loves thee.

You've counted your hopes
As they've gone down the drain,
And you've counted your beans
'Till it drove you insane,
And you suffer injustice
But silence your pain;
But don't worry, my friend,
You'll be heard in the end:
For the Good Lord still loves thee.

You've seen all the carnage
And seen all the hate,
And you've seen tensions rise
At an alarming rate,
And you know there's no end
To the raging debate;
But don't worry, my friend,
You'll find calm in the end:
For the Good Lord still loves thee.

You've lived your life well
And so came to the end,
And there's still just so much
That you can't comprehend,
And you think of the problems
That you could not mend;
But don't worry, my friend,
You've done well in the end:
For the Good Lord still loves thee.

EPITAPH • In the Cemetery

Within that tomb lies Homeless Jack;
He died from smoking too much crack.

And there's clockmaker Sam McKnopt;
He died the day his ticker stopped.

From here we move to Father Blythe;
Saved many souls, yet lost his life.

Up next, we mourn for our pal Ted;
He lost a bet…then, lost his head.

But let's skip over Janie Grist;
So mean, so rude, she won't be missed.

Beneath this stone lies Mrs. Knox;
She died the day she caught the pox.

Let's not forget dear Billy Bread;
He tried to fly, but fell instead.

Pure gluttony killed fat old Drake;
He died from eating too much cake.

Please pay respect to Ann O'Toole;
A bolt of lightning struck her pool.

On hover-boards brave Hayden flew;
Then off he fell, and thus was through.

A smelly death befell Coltrane;
He slid into a sewage drain.

And don't you laugh at dumb old Chris;
His final words were, "Y'all watch this!"

At last, we visit Mara Mood;
She swam with sharks, but died as food.

Epilogue/Moral of the Story

These epitaphs in silence lie,
And grow in length as more folks die.
So while you're living, live life well;
For when it ends, no one can tell.

Please know the dead once lived like you,
And just like them, you shall die, too.
Let not your actions leave you daft,
Or rue what's on your epitaph.

WHAT SMELLY HOMELESS GENTLEMAN

(Set to the tune of "God Rest Ye Merry Gentleman," a Christmas tune)

What smelly homeless gentleman has landed on my stoop?
He reeked of drugs and alcohol; his clothes were stained with poop.
I couldn't leave him in the cold,
The neighbors would all stare;
So I made him take a bath to show I cared, show him I cared!
Yes, I made him take a bath to show I cared.

I woke up in the morning and found all my stuff was gone!
I ran to call the cops, but then I looked upon my lawn.
My homeless man had built a fort,
And he looked quite at home;
Though I noticed he had killed all my lawn gnomes, killed my lawn gnomes!
Yes, my homeless man had killed all my lawn gnomes.

For months that smelly homeless man has really been a pain!
Each moment that I look at him just drives me more insane.
I've reached a realization,
So curse my helpful whim;
He now owns my house and I've turned into him, turned into him!
Yes, he owns my house and I've turned into him.

SO, THERE!

They tried to make me fail,
But I would not accept their plan;
They tried to prove I couldn't,
But I showed them that I can.

They tried to shut my voice up,
But I made them cheer my name;
They tried to drive me out,
But I came back and did the same.

They tried to overwhelm me,
But I rose above the noise;
They tried to rend me foolish,
But I smote their words with poise.

They tried to strip me naked,
But I stopped them in their tracks;
They tried to lock me up,
But I escaped right through the cracks.

They tried to prove me wrong,
But I still proved that I was right;
They tried to win the battle,
But I still survived the fight.

They tried to quell my writing,
But I wrote and did not care;
And they tried to steal this poem,
But I stole it back, SO, THERE!

GOODBYE AND GOOD RIDDANCE

From here,
It is all too clear:
Too long I have hidden
In pointless obsession;
Afraid that if I stepped
Outside of myself,
I would not come back.
But now,
I see with the scales pulled
And opened eyes;
The beauty is so amazing,
I never want to be told
I must go back in the dark.
Ah, to live
Before I found truth,
Away from this freedom,
Back in the dark days
Of depravity,
Anxiety,
Depression,
Loneliness
And distrust;
That is behind me now.
No more excuses,
No more delusions of grandeur,
No more sad regret
For things I cannot change;
I am born anew.
Today, I can rest easy,
Safe from the tormenting temptation
Of that lively caricature,
Depicting the good life
I am told
I should want:
Promising pleasure,
It delivers only dependence.
My life shall be lived
For eternity:
Not here as I am,
Not now, as an empty shell.

I will live the light of salvation.
My mind is made up,
I go with my God.
Send my regards to my sins;
Goodbye and
Good riddance.

THIS RHYME

Hey you.
Yeah, you!
I see you do
What you do
As you live in your life,
Free from strife;
You stay away
From the edge
Of the ledge
Separating me
From the key
To unlock my frustration:
Do you see my situation?
Man, I can't think
With the stink
Of the lies
In your eyes
Day after day,
Chasing me away
From the dreams I desire
Can't you feel the fire?
Like a rod of hot wire,
It burns the shame
Of false fame
That you claim
Makes me lame–
Never mind.
You can't find
What you seek;
You're too weak
To face the facts
That you tax
My individuality:
In reality,
You're fighting lost time
Through the crime
Of all you surmise;
You must rise
Above the bar
Of whom you are,

So I'll tolerate
The rising rate
Of hypocrisy in your smile
For a while;
But now I'm through
So you do
What you do
And let me be me
And look and see
I have no more time
To continue this rhyme…

YEARS OF YOUR LIFE
(For my Red Cap friends, College Freshman Orientation)
Sung to the tune of "(Good Riddance) Time of Your Life" by Green Day

Another session gone,
Another chance to grow;
Advising freshmen,
Telling parents where to go;
We made the best of our quest to make a friend.
We lived the memories, and hoped they would not end.
It's something unforgettable,
This moment framed in time:
Red Caps will be the best years of your life.

So do your mingling,
And waving in the sun;
Dancing on the stage,
Hypnosis was so fun;
Sometimes it rained, but still it never got us down.
Gifts from a secret friend would wipe away our frown.
It's something unforgettable,
This moment framed in time:
Red Caps will be the best years of your life.

It's something unforgettable,
This moment framed in time:
Red Caps has been the best years of my life.

LIKE I USED TO KNOW
(new version from 5-27-04)

In the hard times, I need a reminder
Of the way things were when I was young;
Naïve and neurotic, I never knew if the future
Would reward my efforts, or throw away my memories…

Somebody give me a sign! Anything will do.
Give me something I had, give me another glance
Of something familiar…like I used to know

I have grown since then, while everything was changing.
My life morphed without knowing, but I never really cared.
Though it should have been noticed, I suddenly grew up;
Facing life as I know it, without anything for me to say…

Somebody give me a sign! Anything will do.
Give me something I had, give me another glance
Of something familiar…like I used to know.

When I don't know what's coming, it's scary to know,
But I can make it through; this much is true.

Somebody give me a sign! Anything will do.
Give me something I had. Show me anything familiar;
Please just give me a sign of what I used to know.

SOLDIER ON

When you can't find your place within this world,
And the mysteries just won't be unfurled,
And you can't get your mind to be uncurled,
Soldier on, soldier on.

When you just can't get an ounce of respect,
And you can't help those you vowed to protect,
And you give but all you get is neglect,
Soldier on, soldier on.

When you can't help but feel greatly depressed,
And you try many times but fail the test,
And you know that you're behind all the rest,
Soldier on, soldier on.

Soldier on through the dark of the night,
Soldier on through the pain and the plight,
Soldier on until you see the light,
Soldier on, soldier on.

When you've given your all and still get none,
And you no longer feel you're having fun,
Keep the faith, and one day you'll be the one;
Soldier on, soldier on, soldier on…soldier on.

THE ONLY THING I SAW WAS MY FACE

In a world filled with darkness,
I am the light without a source,
Ready to shine the way;

In a room filled with noise,
I am the only sound you need to hear,
Leading you from the confusion;

In the cold void of everyday life,
I am the laughter lifting your spirit,
So you soar high above the monotony;

In the midst of all the bad news,
I am the escape you dreamed of,
When dreams were all you had;

In the middle of your worst nightmare,
I am the soothing hand on your back,
Promising that it will all work out;

In that moment you were judged by others,
I am the lawyer that told the jury
They could not condemn their own;

In the hour you felt you did not belong,
I am the one that stood by your side,
Because I once stood in your shoes;

In the days that you asked for answers,
I am the one, who knew what to say,
Since I once asked your questions;

In the times you felt you had failed,
I am the one, who dried your tears,
For I knew you would survive.

In the times that I fought your battles,
I am the one, who looked in your eyes,
And, the only thing I saw was my face.

WON MY WAR

The thoughts in my mind spiral,
Spinning, twisting as
I question the truth in life,
Failing, wailing when
I want to believe there is more,
Joking, laughing while
I pretend that I don't care,
Lying, crying until,
I feel better for a little while,
Watching, waiting as;
I hope my failure will stay hidden,
Bleeding, seeing that
I shall be met halfway for once,
Probing, digging when,
I wish you'd leave my mind alone,
Sharing, caring as
I fall on my sword, revealing my honesty,
Wanting, trying since
I want a goal that lies beyond my reach,
Praying, listening and
I wait for my ship to come,
Knowing, feeling that
I want to please, yet still fall short,
Guessing, pressing and
I want answers now,
Leading, reading when
I want only to be understood.
Leaving, breathing since
I can survive anything now,
Fading, jading since
I think the journey is over,
Panting, ranting but
I made it as good as it gets,
Trying, denying that
I said all I could possibly say,
Gasping, rasping since
I fought and won my war.

HIGH AND MIGHTY

It must feel good
To make me feel bad,
But it won't help you to save face
By defacing me;
Admit the truth:
I'm your escape from yourself.
Through mocking me,
Insulting my image,
You are the bigger man,
Heralding your victory
To an audience of only one;
Well, I hate to burst your bubble,
But you are nothing
If your accomplishments involve
Diminishing mine;
There's no place in heaven
For self-glorifying fools;
Why don't you just come down to earth?
Leave your ivory tower,
And join me down here
In humility;
It's actually pretty nice at my level!
I'm just living my life,
Leaving you alone;
Give up on trumping up yourself;
You're living a puny,
Dilapidated little thing
You call a life, so
Stop lambasting the quality
That I ascribe to my own lifestyle;
No one told you to like me,
Or how I view the world,
JUST SHUT UP ALREADY!
I'm tired of proving to you
That I don't care
About what you think,
So think what you will of me.
Go on, now,
Poison yourself with negativity.
It's not me who needs help.

It's you, and only you.
I know that if you had control,
I would be on my knees envying you
In an instant;
That's not going to happen,
No matter how desperate
You happen to be.
But I'll humor you,
I'll let you think that you're winning.
You'll soon see:
You're not so high and mighty.

THE ASPERGER CREED

If I seem a little bit lost, then
Help me to find my way.
If I seem a little bit confused, then
Help me to find understanding.
If I seem a little bit overwhelmed, then
Help me to find some calm.
If I seem a little bit lonely, then
Help me to find some support.
If I seem a little bit awkward, then
Help me to find some inclusion.
If I seem a little bit offended, then
Help me to find a correct response.
If I seem a little bit unaware, then
Help me to find awareness of my situation.
If I seem a little bit off topic, then
Help me to find my train of thought.
If I seem a little bit obsessive, then
Help me to find a distraction.
If I seem a little bit hopeless, then
Help me to find some hope.
If I seem a little bit unsuccessful, then
Help me to find confidence in my talents.
If I seem a little bit helpless, then
Help me to find help for myself.

CAPTAIN ALARM CLOCK

When I moved into my new dorm room,
I could not shake this feeling of impending doom.
And I just did not know why that was,
Then I heard a shrill sound that went beep and went buzz,
And it went beep, beep, beep, beep, beep, beep, beep, beep, beep, beep, beep,
beep, BEEP.
Yes, it went beep, beep, beep, beep, beep, beep, beep, beep, beep, beep, beep,
beep, BEEP!
And I knew in my heart filled with dread,
As the noises rang on in my head,
I lived with Captain Alarm Clock.

The alarm kept on ringing for days,
And I wandered through life in a head-aching haze.
This disturbance just wasn't all right,
Keeping me from my sleep and my work every night,
As it went beep, beep, beep, beep, beep, beep, beep, beep, beep, beep, beep,
beep, BEEP.
Kept going beep, beep, beep, beep, beep, beep, beep, beep, beep, beep, beep,
beep, BEEP!
And I knew that it might be my fate,
I'd go mad if I acted too late,
All thanks to Captain Alarm Clock.

And I think now I'm starting to see
How annoying alarm clocks can be
But that's just Captain Alarm Clock.
What's up with that guy's alarm clock?
Somebody kill that alarm clock!

LEAVING YOU BEHIND

With the walls closed in around me,
There is no escape.
Here, within my mind's prison, I await my captor's advance.
You cannot see him, invisible to your naked eye,
But I see him, lurking still.
I have seen his image all too clearly.
The stamp of Asperger Syndrome brands my soul,
Marking me by my tormentor;
Initials read "AS," ready, set to burn out my life sentence.
What did I do to deserve this fate?
Heaven only knows why I have been bound,
Controlled by Meltdowns and Disorientation;
Don't forget their brothers,
The Infamous Depression and Anxiety,
Those that bedded my senses in the nuptials of disarray
That left me gasping for more:
No more gasping, now.
"Enough is enough" is long overdue.
I'm done begging for peace of mind that's rightfully mine.
You took my body, already had my mind:
Now you want my life, too?
NEVER! Away, demented master!
Leave now; go in peace so I can keep mine.
Or else, I'm leaving you behind.

OBJECTS NOW OF TIMES BYGONE

Farewell, so long,
Objects of times bygone;
How well you served your purpose,
But now, your age betrays you.
Long, long I basked in fantasy, bride of my loneliness!
Like a camel in one of Robert Frost's desert places,
You guided me beyond the threshold.
Passing the coming of age, adulthood found me too soon.
What to do, now,
Where to go, now, objects of times bygone?
Your fantasy no longer bewitches me,
Nor do memories any longer hold my hand;
Years of dedication, all for you;
Now they lie at the bottom of a Connecticut garbage dump:
They've reached the final destination for unloved things.
No twenty-one-gun salute,
No moving memorial service
For you, at long last, objects of times bygone;
Did I let go of you, I wonder, or did you let go of me?
I hold you no more,
Still, you will not quit your hold on me.
Let go of my heartstrings now, my little darlings,
And let me say goodbye, so long,
Farewell, my objects now of times bygone.

DEFINITION OF POETRY

What we call "poetry"
Is to rhyme scheme, you see,
So your words all align
To the beat you assign,
All so patterned to match,
—More than words in a batch—
It is style and prose
That a good writer knows,
Things like rhythm and sense
And like meter and tense,
Which a poet can use
To confound or amuse
With what language they please
About life, God, or bees;
Or all that which inspires
Details; writing requires
To be said in short lines
Feeling rhyme scheme confines,
Like these words which I wrote
In the hope to emote
That good poetry means
More than just hills of beans,
But this poem's too long,
So I hope it's not wrong.

MEMOIRS OF A NATURE HIKE

Cold breeze, a runny nose,
A bad combination, so the old saying goes.
It's allergy season,
And I'm hiking through the woods, for some insane reason.
A friend invited me; I couldn't say no to their request.
"It's beautiful on the mountain in spring," they pressed.
"You'll love it up there!
We've never yet had that experience to share,
And anyway, you don't get out much."
So, I saw the all the flowery blooming shrubbery and such.
Then, my eyes puffed shut;
As my skin broke out in hives, I itched like a nut,
While my nasal passages stuffed up so they felt nonexistent;
But at least I got out of my room for an instant.
And I briefly saw the sights.
So hey, it's better than the walls I see days and nights.
Still, I questioned the experience.
With my intelligence,
I should have gone back to my safe, manmade dwelling
While I could still breathe without itching or swelling,
Oh! If there's a way to divorce a friend,
Please let me know, because the next trip into the woods will be my end.
That's my story, so laugh if you like,
Because I've now suffered twice, in telling you my memoirs of a nature hike.

PROBLEMATIC IAMBIC PENTAMETER

I cannot stand pentameter,
Or each little parameter;
 It's not a thing I care to learn,
And if I try, then up I'll burn!
My problem is I see the way
These youthful poets write today:
They mix up if, and, then, and but,
They mix who, when, where, why, and what,
To make some truly torpid thing,
Or write a song no one would sing;
Still, though I find myself quite scared,
I'll read these works my peers prepared.

ROLLER DROP

SLAM! CRASH! BAM! BONK!
Slip, slide, WHAM! WONK!
Eek, oops, OH NO!
Can't stop, watch, WHOA!
Last bruise, dead stop;
I'll skate until I drop.

SOME THOUGHTS, CRUCIFIED ON THE CROSS WITH CHRIST

When I gaze upon that cross,
The once excruciating abode of a now-risen Lord I call my own,
I forget my failures and rejoice in my confusion
On my knees, I recognize that my yoke has slid from my shoulders,
Into the oblivion I've created.
Here, my torment, oh, my torment,
This mind at odds with itself will sleep for a while, in the calm embrace.
I am no longer couched within myself,
Needing half-hour showers to bath away the stench of failure,
Constantly pervading my every interaction;
Nor do I hear endless recordings of unsuccessful adventures,
Or the countless fictions I believed about my self-image, as
I leave behind my shaky place in life for a moment.
This new freedom is a welcome gift from chains of unnecessary obligation to anxiety,
Along with the bondage of limitation,
Self imposed, inviting darkness;
So, I bow in a new submission,
Requiring only joyful faith rewarded with forgiveness:
This is the best kind of equivalent exchange.
My songs ascend the heavens; I see my shame erased.
It's funny, isn't it, how joy is birthed from a thing as simple as letting go of myself.
And these burdens I can reject as nothing more than some thoughts crucified,
Nailed on the cross beneath the feet of my Lord, with
Jesus Christ, King of my soul.

ONSET OF DEAFNESS
MY BLESSING

VREEP! VREEP! VREEP! VREEP!
This is the sound of sanity collapsing aflame,
Continuous pain, the raining sound oozes over around my eardrums.
Make it stop! Make it end!
Anything to steal back the quiet is yours to take.
I feel my head vibrate in Mezzo Forte;
A regular staccato of torment penetrates the sacred sanctuary,
Tumbling, the walls cave in upon my hallowed halls.
Indiscriminate violation of these ears unwilling
Builds the crescendo to my over-stimulated senses crashing down;
No means no, I screamed in muted terror!
(Apparently, every no is turned into yes upon resounding yes.)
In the flashing lion's eye of your siren apparatus,
We are the sheep, watch us flee before you!
I could see this wave of panic building long before it thundered onto my shore,
Caressing my sense of direction swept out into your riptide;
I've drowned in this black sea before my breath deserted me.
Against logic, I swim around the vibrating insanity,
Wrought from unsuspecting peace
Into an undoing resurrected by transmutations of shame orgies;
But outside, the hellish noise disaffects the world.
I am consigned to wonder why
These temporary alarms to a temporary personal apocalypse go unnoticed:
The onset of deafness will be my blessing.

Poems from Graduate School

(2010-2012)

SEE ME NOW

Glaring at this reflection, I see what I despise:
No self-control, no longer my goal, I walk to my demise.
Walking the wrong direction, my only light is shame:
No salvation for failure done, I see what I've became.

This is not the path I chose, this is not what my heart knows;
This is not the way it goes; this should not, but still, it grows.

Living a life worth doubting should not be life at all;
Yet I'm brought out, paraded about, I stumble on and fall.
There is no more mistaking this fate, which I have wrought;
No more a man, a name in a can, I'm now the fool I thought.

This is not the path I chose, this is not what my heart knows;
This is not the way it goes; this should not, but still, it grows.

Still self-hating, no debating, so frustrating:
This is how I see me now.

Light feels blinding, lies unwinding, not rewinding:
This is how I see me now.

WASTING MY TIME ON YOU

In this ungodly stillness, the confusion comes back to haunt me;
Caressing every synapse of thought,
Playing back today's memories
–Like a bad movie shown for the umpteenth time–
Reminding me to again beg the still inevitable question
Dancing across my twitchy lips:
Why is this simplicity so hard?
Millions of other people are able to get it,
So allegedly simple that even an idiot can figure it out;
The "it" is communication,
And I'm long gone beyond the idiot gate, as my eyes can tell.
They all said that I was perfectly normal,
And my differences were too minor for disclosure.
But the world only ever knows what the world is able to see,
Or else, whatever is convenient.
My poker face is unbroken,
But my insides lay scattered askew.
Is the charade worth it when the curtain comes down?
You see confidence,
The others see a fun quirkiness,
And the majority sees answers to questions that I'll never even know.
If I can't read your intent,
And the only solution is to keep guessing,
Riddle me this, Mr. Joker: Am I just wasting my time on you?

SET TO GREET TOMORROW

Remember, in days of old
When we got lost inside of ourselves
It was so hard to return.
But here we are, standing steady and boldly face the world.
Everybody's waiting, everybody's waving;
They believe in you, just like I believe in you.
Ready, set, stand at the starting line:
Wait for the signal.
Now, forget the old self;
They are history, done and already gone.
Focus only on who you are as I see you in this place,
Face to face, reflecting,
We are ready for what's next.
Ready, set, stand, and greet the day:
Stand bold, stand proud, stand tall against the wind.
You cannot fall if you are steadily supported.
Take note of this moment.
Tomorrow, you might greet us as we waver here,
Full of doubt as we are;
But the fear will vanish if we are there to catch each other.
I can stand forever
So I can wait and wave with you;
I'll hold your hand for now, because
I'm ready, set to greet tomorrow.

TRAPPED NO MORE

In the public's eye, I am seen as the carefree soul,
Filled with boundless joy and dancing;
But that is just my exterior.
My mind is a place filled with gloom and doom,
Overflowing with human distrust for others, for myself;
For every single way I could possibly mess up,
Or that I might have my flaws brought out just when I start feeling confident;
I experience overstimulation galore,
Obsessive-compulsive behavior, depression, anxiety,
And I wonder how I can still have the energy to put my faith in God.
(Humanity only makes this difficult.)
If I know my blessings exist, why do I feel as if I'm a phony?
These questions torment me in tempest beneath my smile,
Along with daily confusion over various happenings and answered questions;
Life seems so clear to others,
While simple details wrack me in mental anguish.
I explained this once to my spiritual mentor, and he said:
"Live in the world, but not of the world."
I think I understand the part about not being of the world,
But being in the world is still no easier.
If things made more sense,
Then this turbulent inner core would match my calm outer shell.
On that day, I can finally stop thinking so much,
And the sun will shine in my soul, attesting to how I am trapped no more.

SUMMER DAYS

The summer is alive,
Full of growth, long relaxed days and lazy heat;
But, as with all seasonal good times,
Summer fades into autumn,
And relaxation fades into a new daily grind.
Though I wish this weren't so,
I must face reality.
This reality says that life works in a cycle
Of birth, growth, new expositions,
Developments of change,
And later, at the last stage of the road,
A pit-stop marked Death awaits all of us, sooner or later.
So it is with summertime,
Ultimately transforming into autumn, then winter,
Breathing fresh life and new possibilities
With warmth-heralding spring;
Therefore, the lesson to be heard is this:
Though the weather turns cold and flowering plants die, fear not.
In the bridging intermission
Between the seasons each of us yearn,
We have time to again anticipate
New seasons of growth, long relaxed days, and lazy heat,
As with each pleasant past time nestled in our memory's bosoms, for
There will be more summer days.

GIVE UP ON THE CHASE

Thinking in pictures, it's hard to grasp the words I can't see.
Growing despondent, your words are less than nonsense to me.
Lost in translation, you are the one who must be confused.
Silenced by your hand, I am the one who won't be abused.

Bow down to this, just so I can save face;
It's just another way to lose the human race:
Accept inferiority…that's not a way I want for me!
I shall not fall; why won't you give up on the chase?

Lost in illusions, it's hard to tell what's truthfully real.
I won't believe you, asking for feelings I cannot feel.
All so uncertain, and yet it's wrong if I wonder why.
This is the reason I cannot let my agony die.

SPOKEN:
"You want me to conform to your empty standards after all I've done to establish myself on my own? Well, the hell if I do. Huh, the fact that you're counting on my cooperation is an insult I won't even dignify. Go and find another victim, fool. I'm done with trying to appease the likes of your kind."

Bow down to this, just so I can save face;
It's just another way to lose the human race:
Accept inferiority…that's not a way I want for me!
I shall not fall; why won't you give up on the chase?

DEATH BY ASSIMILATION

Another broken soul trapped in another hole;
Another person who will never have control;
Caught in the same charade, stepped on your own parade,
Another person won't admit the mess they made.

Lost in bad memories, I cannot hear the melodies
Of lies that we've been sold;
It's starting to get old.
Now that the dreams have died, I'll burn my anger locked inside
And save my destination:
No death by assimilation!

Another path astray, more light gets ripped away;
Another martyr that won't live to see the day;
No longer fit to care, it's all that I can bear
To watch you crumble, then you vanish in midair…

Lost in bad memories, I cannot hear the melodies
Of lies that we've been sold;
It's starting to get old.
Now that the dreams have died, I'll burn my anger locked inside
And save my destination:
No death by assimilation!

BIO POEM THE THIRD

Jim—
Cheerful, confused, and stubborn as hell;
Relative of my family, my circumstances, and all voice actors by way of interest;
Lover of all things holy, fine old cheeses, and Supernatural;
I am one who feels constipated, elated, and occasionally inundated;
I am one who fears ignorance, Los Angeles, and alarm clocks of all shapes and sizes;
I am one who needs attention, laughter, and a better pair of formal footwear;
I am one who would like to see eternity, a miracle, and a fat guy dancing in graceful ballet to Swan Lake;
Resident of both the Here and the Now,
—Madonna

PEDESTAL OF PARADISE LOST

You speak in calm,
Slow tones,
And your eyes wish to belie a gentle intent,
But I cannot deny to myself
That you are where my happiness
Reaches an end:
Oh, succubus of my joy!
It is you,
The emotional vampire,
Creating within my mind
A perfectly beautiful vision of dystopia;
This broken paradise of despair
Exists only by your hand:
My powerlessness is the sweetened nectar
Of your vile efforts,
Reminding me of my tenfold flawed being;
Meanwhile,
You wave your false flag of Normalcy
Expecting me to march in time;
Your expectations evoke only disgust,
As every word brings more distrust;
What do you mean by playing this game?
Has no one told you I have eyes to see?
Your wicked little horns
Are not hidden from me;
No disguise shall suffice for you.
Oh, you that would call me a friend!
I'd rather have an enemy
Presented as being real,
So that I might smite them in a fair fight:
But you are more vicious
In your affections, and
My happiness
Would only breed hopelessness
If you were allowed your way;
But my faith in something greater
Still remains,
Even as my faith in you,
In me, in society
Dwindles into shaky social atheism;

Know this:
I still stand unbroken, unbeaten.
And I am not afraid to face you alone:
Enjoy your reality of broken covenants,
And your endless shame parades:
Your crusade shall fail,
And up again I shall rise.
Fate harkens near to deliver your destiny
Dealing heavily in your defeat;
For you, there is
Naught but a pedestal of paradise lost.

SHADES OF ONLY GRAY

Hey there, Brother Citizen,
Have you heard the news today?
Heard the latest argument
Made to give our hope away?
I think I might go insane
If there's yet another way
To discount validity
Of my every word I say;
You said it will not matter
If the truth is held at bay,
Fooling poor as well as rich,
The noble among the lay;
For all is well that ends well,
But to this I tell ye nay:
We're all the same and human
If we're straight, unsure, or gay;
And surely we shall not live
Long enough to see the day,
When each step ahead demands
Another new way to pay;
But, though it might seem hopeless,
I can only hope there may
Be more to color this life
Beyond shades of only gray…

DON'T EXPECT WONDERS

If I felt better,
Maybe I'd write a poem,
But perhaps later;

Yes, later is good.
Right now, I'm way too busy:
It will have to wait.

What? You want haikus?
Maybe versed rhyme–an epic???
Sir, that is too much!

You must be insane!
I cannot write a poem,
Not with THIS old pen!

Why do you rush me?
I said I can't write a thing.
See? My hand has cramped!

Gosh, you're persistent!
Well, okay…I'll write a bit.
Don't expect wonders.

LEAF DUTY

On fall afternoons during my high school years,
I would go to my pool, already covered for the season,
And I would pick up fallen leaves by hand.
The big ones weren't so bad,
But the little leaves, those tiny freaking little leaves, were so hard to pick up!
Finally, I would be finished, and the wind would blow.
One big leaf would land RIGHT...IN...THE CENTER of the pool,
Beyond the reach of my skimmer;
Oh, I was out there for hours every single afternoon!
I could have been out, at least trying to have an excuse for a social life,
But no, my parents wouldn't allow that.
It was, without a doubt, the worst season of my life to have OCD.
Even my then-driving instructor urged me: "Just let the leaves FALL!"
I did this activity for three consecutive autumns,
And then I went off to college.
I can tell you this:
Falling leaves never looked as beautifully autumnal as they did in freshman year.
It may be because they no longer symbolized the autumn of my sanity.
Later, when I made new friends, I told them about "leaf duty."
They told me I was crazy, or at least that my parents were.
But I ask them this:
Did any of them ever feel the joy of kicking leaves carefree?
Have they ever walked down a campus sidewalk,
Knowing they were *FREE from Leaf Duty?*
...No, I didn't think so.

DIAMOND LEAF POEM

Silently,
Perfectly still,
Treelike I stand,
Unmoving as a statue,
Holding leaves in my hands
Observing the world as living art;
One man, one vision, one with nature,
I become completion as I have never known.
Within this sanctuary, I am free to contemplate life
Without the opinions of others to define my every action;
This leaf becomes my shield, which keeps you out,
Even if my shield is an imaginary barrier;
My muse very often finds me here,
One with the world of nature;
I become one with myself.
At peace, in silence,
I'll abscond again
Into darkness,
Enlightened.

POETIC PROCRASTINATION

Here I sat in silence weeping,
As the night was onward creeping;

On my progress, fate took note
While on I struggled as I wrote;

Thoughts passed within my weary mind,
But once or twice, or so I'd find;

Just then, the clock upon the wall
Made noises loud throughout the hall;

With shoulders slumped, my time was nigh
To kiss this woeful task goodbye;

And from my tear-stained work I parted,
But with sudden halt, I started;

Grinning with a soul most jolly,
I saw knowledge in my folly:

While I worked till nearly dead,
My work was pushed one week ahead!

A COLLECTION OF SHORT POEMS

PROCRASTURBATION

If you use procrasturbation
As a form of recreation,
You'll have fun; I'll give you that.
But all you do beyond...falls flat.

PRACTICAL ADVICE ON POETRY

If you cannot write a poem,
There's an easy thing to do:
Make sure it's not a poem
That has gone and written YOU!

ODE TO A DRUNK

Swagger, stagger, raving drunk;
Why do you smell as a skunk?
The alcohol has got to you,
Or you'd not vomit on my shoe.

MY DUMB LYRICS TO SOMETHING MORE FAMOUS

When you wish upon a star,
Don't stand near a moving car.
A friend did this—his name was Ted,
But no more...since he lost his head.

ENCOURAGEMENT OF A GRUMP

If at first you don't succeed,
Encouragement is what you need:
Then you shall have a brighter day,
...And far away from me, I pray.

'CAUSE IT HAPPENED ...AND IT'S TRUE!

We might say our day is darkest,
But the night is hardly done;
And we still say that it's over,
Though it's only just begun.

We might say that we are free,
But we're enslaved by our own hand;
And we say that we have been there,
Though we still don't understand.

We might keep falling to pieces,
But our hearts are set in stone;
And we like to talk of reason,
Though the reason stays unknown.

We might still believe in heaven,
But we've gone to hell down here;
And we dare to follow orders,
Though the outcome stays unclear.

We might think we have things covered,
But our lives have run amuck;
And we can't admit our failure,
Though we've run through all our luck.

We might fumble as we bumble,
But we grumble all the same;
And we're overwhelmed with problems,
Though there's more than we could name.

We might call it all malarkey,
But it could happen to you;
And consider this fair warning,
'Cause it happened...and it's true!

TRUST

An addiction's like a virus,
Since there's nothing you can do;
You live your life, and suddenly
It's taken over you.

It might be an activity,
Or a substance you abuse;
It takes all that you love, until
There's nothing left to lose.

You might try to make excuses,
You might try to wait it out;
But you're living in denial:
Your problems leave no doubt.

Yet, you tell us there's no problem,
Everything's within control;
You've lost your resolution, and
You sacrificed your soul.

Now, it's too late to start over,
Since your dreams have turned to rust;
This could have been avoided, but
You never learned to trust.

YOU CAN'T CRITIQUE
THE CRITICS

They'll tell you to be silent
If they don't like what you say;
They'll keep you out of print
If they cannot get their own way;

They'll chop you into pieces
If you're more than they can chew;
They'll criticize your style
If it gives them more to do;

They'll ebb away your passion
If it leaves you just a shell;
They'll take away your heaven
If it makes your life a hell;

They'll throw you on the fire
If it burns away their shame;
They'll leave you in the dust
If it will help increase their fame;

They'll only cease complaining,
If you play their little game:
 You can't critique the critics;
…If you do, they'll do the same!

NOT FOR YOU...BUT ME!

Spark my anger, burnt with shame;
Tell the world that I'm to blame.
Take my calm, erode my pride;
Give me rules I can't abide.

Hold me captive, bring me out;
Show my failure and my doubt.
Tell the world, go tell them all;
Tell them that you saw me fall.

Say you're sorry, say I'm fine;
Say your same old sorry line.
I was stupid, I was wrong;
You had said that all along.

More defeated, year by year;
Now there's nothing more, I fear.
Make the effort, cut my loss;
This will prove that you're the boss.

Same old story, same old rut;
You're still acting like a nut.
Never winning, still I lose;
No escaping from your ruse.

Once away, I thought this through;
I don't care to challenge you.
Shut the door, and now I'm free;
I'll make things as they should be.

Had your chance, got in my space;
You would not get off my case.
Done my time, my cross to bear;
Now I realize I don't care.

Find your stooge, another tool;
Exercise your right to rule.
But I'm done, so let it be;
My life's not for you...but ME!

ALL I FELT WAS ILL

Once again I sit fixated
By a thought I've instigated
From an image I had seen,
Awash on my computer screen;

Like so many long before it,
–Many made my reason forfeit–
I felt urged to quell my lust,
Or else, I thought, I may well bust.

Still, there was no satisfaction
In my mind's obsessed reaction:
Empty pleasure, this it bore.
Empty pleasures, not much more;

Thus my days went past, time ticking,
–My resolve had long ceased sticking–
The hours passed, I barely knew;
And apprehension dawned anew.

Yet, on I ventured past my doubt,
'Till at long last my time ran out:
I did at last receive my fill,
But inside, all I felt was ill.

A FEW MESSED-UP FAIRY RHYMES

I.

Hickory-dickory-dock;
the mouse ran up the clock.
Too bad there was a mousetrap on top of the clock.

II.

Jack and Jill ran up the hill to fetch a pail of water.
Jack fell down, and broke his crown,
And Jill sued the well-maker after.

III.

Little Miss Moffat sat on her tuffet, eating her curds and whey.
Along came a spider, and sat down beside her,
He then said, "Move your tuffet THAT way!"

IV.

If you wish upon a star, be sure it's not a plane up far.
The moral here that you may miss, is think ahead before you wish.

V.

Never smile at a crocodile; never tip your hat and stop to talk a while.
It's just common sense, but here I digress.
Just don't do it, or you'll come back in a chewed-up pile.

PUT MY SHOES BACK ON

Who are you?
They ask in arrogant irritation,
Pointing their loaded,
Double-barreled questions
At the temple of my soul:
I face my questioner
At eye-level,
And I respond proudly:
I am he who seeks
The seeker of the lost;
I am the atypical antichrist
In your anti-religion of hate
For the abnormal;
You are afraid of what you see.
I said, YOU…ARE…AFRAID
Of what you feel,
Afraid to see
Your reflection might be real;
You might not be typical at all.
And you fear that.
You fear that you might be wrong,
And my atypical views
Might be more humane
Than your normalcy
You think you have,
But you don't.
Guess what?
None of us are normal.
Your normalcy IS…A… ILLUSION
 Pointed at me
To shoot down your fear:
Go ahead,
And shoot words from your mouth;
I can take it.
You could too,
If you took responsibility
For everything you aim to become…
Speaking of which,
Forrest Gump once said
That his momma always told him

He could never understand someone
Until he walked a mile
In their shoes;
His shoes are too big for me.
They're all worn out
From running all day long,
And mine are giving me blisters.
So how about this:
When you want to talk to me
As my equal,
I'll put my shoes back on.

BIO POEM THE FOURTH

Jim–
Silly, seriously spiritual, and scrumptious on occasion;
Relative of the creative, the disabled, and anyone who needs a hug;
I am a lover of action movies, comedy, and really tight superhero costumes;
I am one who feels uncomfortable in crowds, embarrassed when I break wind, and very happy to be here;
I am one who fears germs, pointless chaos, and the sound of a fire alarm;
I am one who needs attention from my peers, food for thought, and reassurance of my sanity;
I am one who would like to see Five Finger Death Punch live in concert, talking cars, and the cast of Jersey Shore go anywhere that isn't on my TV;
Resident of the modern age whether I like it or not,
–Madonna

MY HAT STAYS BLACK

This hat is black.

When the pigs and the preps all deserve a good smack,
This hat, my hat, is black.

When the least and the different are pushed to the back,
And the sharks and the vultures are on the attack,
This hat, my hat, is still black.

When the liars and the lifers are leading the pack,
And the words of the world stick me sharp as a tack,
And they say that the good times are not coming back,
This hat, my hat, continues to be black.

When the haters and harpies slip in through the crack,
And the house of the hopeful is only a shack,
And the critics and crackpots stuff me in the sack,
And good folks understanding have reached a great lack,
This hat, my hat, remains black.

When the experts and know-it-alls call me a hack,
And the ones who care less throw my words on the rack,
And the people in power won't give change a whack,
And the wolves, dogs, and demons gulp me down as a snack,
And those things called "important" aren't really worth jack,
This hat–MY hat–stays BLACK!

This Poem Written in Loving Memory of My Old Black "JIM" Hat: Worn June 2009-
Aug. 2011

LIMERICKS (YOU'LL FORGET ANYWAY)

A poem is much like a fart:
Neatly packaged, it can be an art.
But to some it may smell,
And of this you can tell,
Since away from the source they will dart…

A story is much like perfume:
Its mere presence can fill up a room.
But oh, woe if it's bad,
Or much joy will be had,
When the teller is sent to their doom…

A riddle is much like a joke:
For they both can much laughter provoke.
But there's not much to do,
If the target is you,
And, it's not just some other poor bloke…

A message is much like a day:
It arrives, but again goes away.
If the content is good,
You'll recall what you should,
But if not, you'll forget anyway.

DON'T MAKE ME WRITE YOU A POEM TODAY

I wanted to write you a poem today,
But alas, I just simply could not find a way.
I'm feeling a bit out of sorts on this day,
And a poem might keep my relaxing at bay.
Oh, why must I write you a poem today?
I simply have nothing poetic to say.
Don't make me write you a poem today,
Each part of me screams out in protest, "No, NAY!"
If you can still write out a poem today,
I can only offer a feeble hooray.
And why should I write you a poem today;
I already wrote a good one yesterday!
It's possible I'll write a poem today,
About a bookmark that I drew up today,
And that bookmark could not write a word anyway,
So I guess this assignment is just not okay.
Go ask someone else to write poems today,
My writer's block won't disappear until May,
Like snow-flooding streets that have long since turned gray;
They're gray like the words I am writing today.
And frankly, I think you should just go away.
Now I've said to you all I wanted to say,
…And I STILL will not write you a poem today!

THIS ISN'T A POEM, AFTER ALL

This is only a poem
If you think it's a poem;
You say that this isn't a poem?
Do you think I'm just lazy?
That I'm simply deceiving you in rhyme
So you think I'm a poet,
Delighting myself in the delusion
When, I'm clearly not,
But still glad you don't know it?
Is THAT what you think?
Shame on you!
Of course I'm a poet.
But what is a poet, or, for that matter,
What IS a poem, you ask?
Well, what is your definition of "IS"?
That is the question, here.
This is an exercise in literary writing,
Not an attack on my character;
Don't be silly,
Of COURSE I intended to write this poem—
—Unless you think I didn't.
I'm pretty sure I'd know a poem if I saw one:
Oh wait…never mind.
This isn't a poem, after all.

LIMERICKS FROM THE LOONY
BIN (An Effort of Two Unnamed Inmates)

The Hover-board
By William L. Stull, Ph.D.
Hover, hover little board;
I'm so glad you're not a Ford.
If you were, I'd trade you in,
Or, go straight to the loony bin!

Limerick for Lilith
By William L. Stull, Ph.D.
There once was a demon named Lilith.
To tell her vile deeds it would filleth
A volume so thick,
It would outweigh a brick;
For this Lilith had willeth to killeth.

Kimblee in the Chimney
By Jim Madonna, MA '12
A fellow who called himself Kimblee
Once found he was stuck in a chimney!
His friend lit a fire,
And caused him much ire,
So nimbly Kim flew out the chimney!

Venus, the Goddess of Love
By Jim Madonna, MA '12
The goddess of love was named Venus.
We flirted, and you should have seen us!
I'd tell you the rest,
But it's hard to suggest
Nothing sexual came up between us.

Limerick for a Professor
By Jim Madonna, MA '12
There was a professor named Stull.
His classes were terribly dull.
His students rebelled,
So he yelled, "Go to Hell!
You're driving me out of my skull!"

Demonic Limerick
By William L. Stull, Ph.D.
A wicked cute devil named Devon
Conspired to raise Hell up in Heaven:
"I'll invent four new sins,
And then when I get in,
I'll open a 7-Eleven."

Limerick of the Loonies
By William L. Stull, Ph.D.
Two loonies escaped the asylum,
Where doctors had carelessly filed them;
They left for a snack,
And then when they came back,
Two LOONIER loonies replaced them!

SIX ODD POEMS

A Sidewalk Neatly Lined
If someone's poem you do find
Upon your sidewalk neatly lined,
Start reading and you'll surely find
The writer may have lost their mind
In thinking you are surely blind,
That you won't notice or else mind
Their poem left for you to find
There on your sidewalk, neatly lined.

Poem on a Stair
A poem written on a stair
Should be trod upon with care
If you can see that one is there,
So other people can all stare,
Before they travel off to where
They'll all be pulling out their hair,
Thinking not without despair:
Why's a poem on my stair??

Poem Written on a Rock
There once was a rock;
It had quite a lock
On the fine art of rhyme,
But it had no time
To write just one verse,
Before it was cursed
By the falling of rain;
So it started again.

Which Is It...A Vandal, Or a Poet?
If in your traveling you see
A rock with metered poetry,
Such as this one which claims to be
A vandal's thoughtful effigy,
Don't wait for an apology,
Or sulk in silent apathy;
One fact you miss, and it's the key:
The vandal didn't write for thee!

A Poem Replaced the Snow
A smooth rock in the sunny spring
Has been through almost everything;
Though snow once graced its stony face,
Behold! A poem takes its place!

Poem from Another Page
Poems, poems everywhere,
But not one makes me think;
I daresay all these poems
For the most part...plainly stink!

IF THEY ONLY LISTENED

This is how you participate
In the neuro-typical person's conversation:
They think that I try to talk with them
Because I enjoy their inclusion,
When, in fact,
I try because their noises are too many
And their noises overwhelm me;
But it is inconvenient for them
To hear my struggle:
No motivation,
No sense of direction,
No ability to contribute any dialogue;
This is what they think
When they see me slouching here,
Sitting in my seat, not contributing–
–But I am contributing.
I am trying to listen,
Because that is all I can do;
I can't fight their noise or shut it up.
So I sit, and I pretend to be one of them,
Like a normal young adult
Without sensory discriminating ears:
But I know the truth.
They could too…if they only listened.

BECAUSE I COULD NOT SPARE ANY MONEY, I GLADLY SOLD MY BODY PARTS, ONE AT A TIME

(ALTHOUGH YOU ASK FOR ANSWERS, I'LL SURELY NEVER TELL)

Because I could not spare any money,
I gladly sold my body parts,
One at a time:
They were already paid for,
So it didn't matter anymore
Whether they were used by me or another;
Thus, I sold my hands
To an artist without fingers to hold a pencil,
And I sold my feet
To a man that doctors said could never walk;
I sold my legs—
They went to a man who had never run.
I extended the use of my arms,
So someone else could hug their family;
I sold my torso—
The receiver had been all arms and legs.
My manhood went to another man:
He, previously, had no balls to face life.
In addition to that,
I gave my mind to Science;
Hence, others could learn from my mistakes.
I settled for sending my stomach
Off to a man with a weak constitution;
My bladder I gave to a child,
So he could sit through school each day;
My ears went to a deaf man,
So he could sit back and enjoy the music;
My eyes went to a blind old beggar,
So he could see how to turn his life around;
My nose went to a man with no smell
So he could appreciate his garden better,
And my tongue was used by a muted man,
That he may tell his story…

I sold these parts of me and many others,
And I also gave my heart to God,
But that happened three years ago.
All I have left is my head,
Though I'll likely lose it soon enough.
So you must wonder:
How then did I write this poem?
I had no stomach for passionate wordplay,
Or a mind for rhyme,
Or a heart for earthly feeling,
Or legs to let my imagination run wild,
Or fingers to tap out a beat,
Or the balls to share myself like this;
It begs many more questions,
But, although you ask for answers,
I'll surely never tell.

I, AT LAST, HAVE PEACE

I've never known such joy as I do now,
Having weathered my season of self-battered separation;
So many things stood between me and the blessing of your love;
I was lost inside, distracted by worldly things;
They were things so mundane they seem ridiculous in retrospect, but not at the
time;
Oh yes, it seemed much more important for me to wonder:
Why is my computer so slow?
How did I screw up my DVD player at 1 A.M.?
Will I ever attract a woman, and get to enjoy sweet physical love with her?
Do my secrets make me a bad person or a bad Christian?
Am I nothing more than the limitations of my Asperger Syndrome?
Will I ever be at peace with my past or myself?
AM I SELFISH FOR ASKING THESE QUESTIONS???
But now I know that these questions neither matter nor do they define me;
The struggles of my life have always been in God's hands,
Those wonderful hands, pierced on the cross to free me from my sins;
I know with confidence that I am undeniably free.
I am unbound by my past, my flaws, my sins, my failures, my limitations, my
thoughts—
All of those things were long since forgiven, even when I couldn't forgive
myself.
The amazing grace and love of my Lord and Savior is in control.
He has always been in control, even when I refused to acknowledge Him;
But He is there, He loves me, and in Jesus Christ I am free.
In His Hands I am free, I am strong, and I am confident, competent,
And best of all, I am well.
Because I know the Truth, I, at last, have peace.

THE HERO OF THE FIREHOUSE
(In Loving Memory of Kyle J. Cofiell, 1987-2011)

He is the hero of the firehouse,
Beloved by all, companion of many, a celebrity in his time;
And yet, he's never felt so alone.
The hero of the firehouse has lead an unselfish life,
But for once, he's decided to be more selfish than anyone around him can dare
to accept.
He feels the rough texture of the rope tied around his neck, and
He sees his world collapsing invisibly around him, and
He can already feel the fires that will be eternally fighting HIM in the next
world,
And he can already hear the judgment rendered against him,
But the hero of the firehouse no longer cares.
In his line of work, he half believes that he won't be long for this world,
And he knows that the expectations people hold for him don't belong in this
world.
But he is the hero of the firehouse,
And that's exactly how he wants people to remember him.
He thinks about his friends over at the university.
He thinks about what his family will say.
Mostly, the hero of the firehouse thinks about his own inner pain,
Never seeing that he had a chance to be understood;
But he is the hero of the firehouse, and in his mind, his burden is his to bear
alone.
He takes one last look around at the world he knew so well,
And he briefly regrets the lasting sorrow he knows his decision will cause;
But his mind is made up, and it has been for a while.
The hero of the firehouse takes one last breath, preparing himself for his great-
est feat yet.
Then, the former hero of the firehouse steps bravely off, into oblivion.

A BRANDED MESS OF MEMES AND TAGLINES

A dude told me I should've bought a Dell,
But I run on Dunkin,
As does America,
So I was glad to learn I'm in good hands with Allstate.
Though I just kept going, and going, and going,
There was comfort in knowing
I could eat great, even late, at Taco Bell.
This way,
I can come hungry but leave happy, because
I'll find rest, on the wings of Lunesta;
After all, why would I want to keep up with the Kardashians?
Last I checked I'm (DUH!) winning!
My university's president told me not to be a knucklehead.
I won't be a knucklehead,
Since switching to Geico can save me 15% or more on car insurance.
You don't need to hide your kids,
Hide your wife,
Or hide your husband;
Choosy moms choose Jif,
And the quilted, quicker picker-upper:
Knowing those things has become so obvious,
Even a caveman can do it.
The Decider once said
A quirky old man told him more flags mean more fun.
If that's true, I'm on a boat
Singing, "I'm never gonna give you up, never gonna let you down…"
Out there, Donald Trump can't tell me, "You're fired."
Are you cuckoo for Cocoa Puffs?
My Lucky Charms are magically delicious.
I'm not a witch,
And I didn't bring change we can believe in.
Anyway—oh my God, they killed Kenny!
That's hot,
Like a hockey mom from Alaska.
Maybe he didn't trust the girly men to whom
The Governator told his true lies.
Forrest Gump said life is like a box of chocolates;
You never know who will be the biggest loser,
Or working in The Office
At the Jersey Shore.
Oh, very well.
The only option is to become an American Idol:
—Unless, of course, I'm unable to just do it.

SIX MORE LOONY POEMS

• Rambling Randall

There once was a boy known as Randall.
When he spoke, on and on he would ramble.
Then he swallowed a fly,
And that might explain why
It's his buzzing that's harder to handle!

• The Cleaning Ninja

There's ne'er a Scrap hast lain betwixt
Thy Broom and Thee what was not nixed;
Oh, Litterers! Put off thy glee!
Thy Cleaning Ninja waits for Thee!

• The Idiot

Oh idiot, oh idiot, oh what will you do?
Oh idiot, oh idiot, you haven't a clue.
Oh idiot, oh idiot, now what have you done?
The idiot, the idiot has ruined our fun.

Oh idiot, oh idiot, now where will you go?
Oh idiot, oh idiot, how little you know.
Oh idiot, oh idiot, oh how can this be?
The idiot, the idiot...has outsmarted ME!

• Study Buddy

It's good that I don't see my buddy:
With my buddy, I'd likely not study.
I'd waste all our time,
Writing riddles in rhyme;
And my grades would be horribly cruddy.

• The Poem I Found in My Closet

A poem was found in my closet today,
All dusty, quite musty, cobwebbed and gray;
And since it is clean, may it not be forgot—

But now that it's written, it surely shall not.

•   The Loony

A loony came from Timbuktu,
And now he's stuck to me like glue.
I really don't know what to do
About this man from Timbuktu;

He hops just like a kangaroo,
And hopped right up the chimney flue;
But looking from his high up view,
He spied another loony...YOU!

SINGING IN THE SHOW

The auditorium is filled to capacity;
There are so many talking heads that
It's hard to tell who is or isn't important.
Finally, one of the emcees walks to the front of the stage.
At his appearance, all is silent.
Then, he speaks to the throngs, straightening his clip-on tie:
"Welcome to the last concert of the year!"
Applause from the audience,
Then it's broken by singing.
I watch from my stolen front row seat:
The boys in the a cappella group have really improved this year,
And the girls look ravishing in all of their glittery, glitzy high-heeled youthful
glory.
I guess it's true what they say,
That the songs of youth are the most beautiful...
Number after musical number washes over me;
When the end comes,
It's hard to believe how much time has really passed.
After the stage clears and the rounds of applause die,
The singers pause to accept compliments from their many adoring peers,
So that I am forced to utter some incoherent praise
Before I am shoved to the back of the line;
The reception is no better.
What with so many conversations going on at once,
Where do I find the right one in which to take part?
Failing to find festive companions,
And fearing that I'll only end up packing my face
With snacks when social skills desert me,
I leave the a cappella group's after-party feeling frustrated;
I bet socializing with my alleged peers would be easier were I the one on stage,
People admiring my performance—
But my only venue is the shower tub in my apartment,
And my only fan is my shower head;
When an audience is that small and unseeingly loyal,
I can't get a bad review;
But there are certainly those times when I watch a play or singing performance,
And I admit with some level of personal guilt,
I am not clapping for their outstandingly skillful talent.
Rather, I am clapping for a fantasy,
One that is uniquely mine:

I am the one on stage,
Hitting every note perfectly as the crowd demands an encore;
Then I wake from my blissful pipe dream.
I am still in the shower, rather than at the front of some mythical chorus line.
One day, I hope to be singing in the show.

STAY TRUE

Did you hear?
They said the end was near.
But we're all still here,
I fear.

Did you know?
They said we'd have great woe.
But there is still no,
To show;

Did they say?
I heard we'd leave today.
But they all said nay:
Hooray.

Did they see?
The future's still to be.
But they don't agree
With me;

Why this rhyme?
The bells have yet to chime.
But here is the crime:
No time.

Why such waste?
You really should make haste.
Or, what you will taste
…Is paste?

Is this dumb?
What have these words become?
As spoken by some:
Ho-hum.

Are you done?
You're not making this fun.
But I've just begun,
So run.

Am I through?
I still won't change for you.
Here is what I'll do:
Stay true.

DIFFERENCE HAS COME TO AMERICA'S DREAM

I can tell what's in the air:
A new tide comes this way.
Difference is coming,
It's come here to stay.
And try as you might,
You can't keep it at bay:
Yes, difference has come,
To America's way—

There's a sound in the air,
One that has its own beat;
It sweeps through the alleys,
And seeps down the street,
As it rips out the chaff
From the rest of the wheat—
Yes, difference has come,
Right there under our feet.

Now, the older folks claim
That the signs can't be right—
They do not hear the battle,
Once caught in the fight.
They're all sitting scared
Till the end of the night;
Yes, difference has come.
And, it shines a new light.

Yes, I've heard people talk:
They don't say what they mean.
And I've been turning blue,
As the whole world goes green;
The damned may well die,
But please do save the scene—

Yes, difference has come
To fatten the lean,
And to count every bean,
And to burst every seam,
And to flatten,
And ream—

Yes, difference has come:
Yes, now it has come to America's dream.

A PARABLE FOR THE OBNOX-IOUSLY RICH AND STUPID

A man of great wealth
But of poor mental health
Got his kicks when he made others frown–
Then, a wise man told him
If he heeds every whim,
He would get himself kicked out of town.

He replied, "You are wrong,
So just move right along."
And he sneered with contempt, feeling snide.
But it was not yet late,
When he met the same fate
As the wise man who sat just outside;

He exclaimed, "Look at me!
You must hate what you see,
When compared to my former renown!
I don't *think* I'm a jerk,
Though I've more than one quirk,
Yet I find I've been kicked out of town!"

The wise man replied,
"Oh, I tell you I've tried,
But you just will not hear what you're told!
You must hold no regret,
Or, you've grown dumber yet,
For your words are still brutish and bold."

The wealthy man cried,
"Well, I'd rather have *died*
Than to hear THIS while down in the dumps;
But still now I can feel
My unfairness was real:
I believed that the townsfolk were chumps."

The wise man then smiled.
"Well, although you're reviled,"
He began, as he nodded his head,
"You don't need to cry,
And I'll tell you just why:
They'll ignore ME if *you're* here instead!"

THE WORLD HAS GROWN AWAY FROM ME

This world has gone confusing
In its ways,
And despite the many contradicting
Reasons I should not abide,
You would have me follow its will.
I try to obey–
And believe me,
I really do!
But still,
I'm lost in the un-logic
Of another catch 22:
Damned if I do,
Damned if I don't,
And most damned
If I choose
Some better third option;
Or, in your case,
It is like this:
You provide for me
An implied expectation,
Then I should follow it without question.
(This is because of
An unrealistic expectation to
"Be like most people"
Meaning,
I should pick up on
Cues for implied instruction)
But guess what, honey…
BIG surprise!
I was born without this
Equally useful and mystifying skill;
So, you leave your instructions
Vaguely implied,
I fail to pick up on your implications,
My failure will annoy you:
Finally,
I think less of myself and
Reaffirm my place as "Damaged."
Repeat steps one through four
As needed,
Wash, rinse,
And dry
Until properly and fully destroyed.

What do you hope to achieve?
Aren't I already inept in spades?
If you want better functioning results
Out of me,
Sweetheart,
You're going to
Need a change of expectations.
Or, if you're not willing to do that,
Hear me explain how my mind works,
For once;
Maybe,
God forbid,
You'll understand me.
Now,
You can keep your expectations,
Ignorant though they were,
As my way of doing things
Produces BETTER results
With which you'll be happy—
Believe it or not,
I'm trying desperately to
Work WITH you.
How about actually trying to
Work with ME?
My faith in the world
Can't possibly get any lower;
And maybe
My faith in you will grow.
But, maybe
I'm only being wasteful
In my wishful thinking—
Yet again, it's true.
If you want to tell me more about
How my thinking is wrong,
—As you illogically proclaim
Denial of the subtlety
I can see clearly in your actions—
Take a number and get in line.
You'll be there a while,
Considering
How long it has grown already…
You do that,
And I'll try to tell myself
It is a lie that
The world has grown away from me.

A FEW RECENT POEMS, TITLED BEGINNING WITH THE WORD "THE"

1. The Candy Stand

A sugar-craving obese man
If placed upon a diet plan
Should not go to the candy stand,
Because once there, you understand;
Entrenched among the sugared sweets,
He'll get sick, as he eats…and eats.

2. The Un-Poem

A bunch of words is only a poem
If it is defined by a poet as a poem;
However, this is definitely not a poem.
It is merely a bunch of words arranged as a poem.
But you are still welcome to enjoy another poem.
And perhaps, that poem will have more rhyming words than "poem."

3. The Poet and the Chainsaw

A poet thought he'd give up rhyme
In hoping he might save some time
To juggle chainsaws, but instead
He writes his rhymes without his head.

4. The Word of the Bird

A paper was left without word,
When a poet left rhyme to his bird.
But it pooped on the page,
And the poet, in rage,
Wondered, why had he been so absurd?

5. The Insect on My Stair

Little insect on my stair:

You do not fly, as birds in air.
You do not buzz, as does the bee,
You're really kind of strange to me.
Your coloring seems blue–or green,
Or maybe brown is what I mean.
Oh, now I know! It's clearly soot–
But now, you're squished beneath my foot.

SAY WHAT YOU MEAN

There are some days where
I'd like to get away from all the noise,
Away from human contradiction,
And the God-awful
Racket of normality;
That's right.
I just don't get the ways of others.
Though many people party for hours on end,
And others prefer
Big, noisy gatherings,
And still others are amused by meaningless profanity,
I don't fit the bill
In any of those categories–
I find myself at wit's end
At the end of a typical workday as a busboy,
And that's hardly socially demanding!
Yet, I see problems
In the ways normal folks deal in communicating:
They are too nice,
When, really,
Frankness is that much more needed.
Though I be a heretic
For suggesting solutions to this highly valid problem,
I cannot fairly follow your rules
If you never tell me that
They exist.
Sadly, this is the norm.
Kindness is given without regret,
Knowing that any
Hidden meanings will be understood.
But I don't work that way.
I'd rather you share with me a bluntly rude truth
Than ambiguous politeness;
I tell you this,
And you think
I'm only being a bother,
Or else I am refusing to admit I am wrong.
However,
I am actually agreeing with you,
And I am attempting to accommodate your request.
Honestly,
How can I please you?
You won't even say what you mean!

SOME POEMS, CONCEIVED WHILST I SWEPT A RESTAURANT FLOOR

• Fireworks from My Dog's Point of View

Oh, to be
A dog as thee
In times of celebration,
Where *Pop! Boom! Bang!*
And wayward *Clang!*
Cause naught but consternation;
Whilst we partake
And joyous make
Ourselves in boundless wonder,
You lie instead
Beneath the bed—
And quake until it's over.

• Whatever Became of the Weather?

Whatever, if ever,
Became of the weather,
That now it must rain all the time;
It surely quite early
Left me feeling surly,
That I'm in such pain so I rhyme!

• My Response to the Poem in "V for Vendetta"

They bid me remember
The fifth of November,
The treason, plot, violence, whatnot—
They asked if I'd ever
Forget; I yelled, "Never!"
But like it or not, I forgot.

• Cursed, if You Can't Tell

I said I'd write just one more verse,

And now things can't get any worse:
With every line I try to type
It's lost again in one quick swipe.
In fact, I'm up to my last nerve,
Believing that I might deserve
To have my efforts shot to Hell—
But now I'm cursed, if you can't tell.

SIX POEMS FROM THE SCRAP HEAP

• Demon Bookmark

I made a demon bookmark,
And as far as I can tell,
I still can say my artwork
…Hasn't fallen straight to Hell!

• Random Writing

Random writing on a page
Isn't hard for one to gauge;
If you look for funny rhyme,
It will never waste your time!

• Fill the Empty Space

This paper must be filled,
So the emptiness is killed
With the writing of my pen,
And it won't be filled again.

• The Busboy

If your current line of work
Makes you crawl beneath your skin,
Then you might just change your mind
When you hear the job…I'M in!

• The Lurking

What lurks beneath, the mind
Of men, I dare not like to know:
But sure as I can help it,
That's one place I'd dare not go!

• In Protest of Language

Don't hate my language for my words,
For though it might seem for the birds,
I only speak to gain reply,
Though you protest, "No more, oh why?"

BIO POEM THE FIFTH

Jim—
Thoughtful, philosophical, and self-aware;
Relative of Italians (NOT the "Jersey Shore" kind), anime fans, and the socially obtuse;
Lover of storytelling, peanut butter, and funny jokes;
I am one who feels vindicated, validated, and thankfully not over-stimulated;
I am one who fears creeper people, creeping idiocy, and walking into a classroom without wearing any pants;
I am one who needs food, hugs, and a good laugh always—oh! And great bushy beards!
I am one who would like to see Jersey Shore be about the shore itself, alchemy to become real, and a live moose;
Resident of my own imagination,
—Madonna

POETICALLY UNWANTED

Oh, your figure is repulsive
And your face does make me spew,
Yes, your smell leaves me convulsive;
How we met, I never knew.

Your bad manners are a horror,
And your grace does sorely lack:
And your social skills are poorer
Than a cat on the attack;

If I could I would restrain you,
Since upon me you do cling;
And those boundaries you pooh-pooh?
You insist that's not your thing.

You are crazier than sin, oh yes,
With speech profane and odd;
And sometimes I must confess
I'd gladly beat you with a rod!

Of the words that fit you strongly,
Perhaps "horrible" is best:
And I do not speak so wrongly:
Your affections I protest.

You are lower than the lowest form
Of life yet known to man,
While your breath is as a firestorm—
No wonder others ran!

How I wish that I would lose you,
And you'd go far, far away;
But although *I* did not choose to,
It appears you're here to stay.

DAMN THIS WRITER'S BLOCK!!!

I decided that today would be the day
I wrote my poetic masterpiece.
Unfortunately, I had no pen.
This one was borrowed, obviously.
By the time I had a means of writing anything,
I had nothing to write;
Well, this stinks.
How will I look my professor in the eye?
I just know that he'll ask me to read
The things I've been writing;
He always does.
I'll probably smile, and then I'll offer to read
Another work I wrote earlier–
There are over 200 from which to choose.
Or, more likely,
I'll pull some verse out of my rear end,
And thus I'll call it poetic art.
(I think the artist Marcel Duchamp did this
Using his home toilet on a pedestal,
Or, at least he stole a urinal from the studio bathroom.)
Maybe, no one will notice.
This works for Bart Simpson every episode of "The Simpsons."
Oh, never mind.
That hardly ever works out at all!
But then again,
Bart is a fictional yellow prankster boy,
A boy with a sizable overbite
Typical of his little universe;
I'm not nearly as creative as him.
And it would take nothing short of a miracle
If these words were enough…
All right, then; I've been writing for a while now,
And my hand has cramped sufficiently,
So I guess that's proof of effort.
Too bad with all these words
There's no substance worthy of sharing.
Oh no, the professor is looking again!
At least he's smiling.
This time, NO! He's calling on me to read my poem!
I still don't have a poem,
So it's time to face my failure, and take the fall.
Why today, of all days, must I draw a blank?
DAMN THIS WRITER'S BLOCK!!!

TAKE ANOTHER TRY AT IT (DAMN THIS WRITER'S BLOCK, PART II)

I've tried all day,
But still, I have nothing.
At least I won't be called on to read again.
Why can't I just write a poem?
I wish I could just get this done,
So I'll be left alone.
Damn this writer's block.
It still hasn't gone away.
Not even three bowls of homemade soup,
Two water bottles,
One Coca Cola,
A Hawaiian punch,
Six trips to the bathroom,
And a very interesting discussion or two
Within the space of a few hours could inspire me;
I can't even write one word.
Oh, look at that…
Now I've got a headache, to boot.
I should have just gone home,
Rather than face my decidedly poetic injustice
Twice, in one day;
Seriously, sir!
How can you expect flowing rhyme out of me?
I'm in graduate school, gosh darn it!
I already DID the poetry thing!
At least, let me escape.
But there's no such luck of that happening.
What am I, some kind of poetry dispenser?
Am I a moo-cow, a set of literary udders you can milk for verse?
No sir, I do not think so.
You make too much demand of me.
The best I can do is one verse:
> *"Roses are red,*
> *And I'm feeling blue…"*
GAH! Do you see what I mean?
I can't even finish someone else's poem,
Not with the right lines, at that.
No matter how much you want to wheedle,
Or needle,
Or make me take lecture from a former Beatle,
I simply shall not–no, shall definitely NOT
Take another chance at this, that is,
Take another try at it.

THE LOVERS' NEST OF SAND

Two lovers
Of untold youth
Nestle together in their secret place.
They think they are hidden
From the world around them:
One friend buries another in the sand nearby
While his buddies swap stories,
Laughing all the while
About some crazy fishing trip recently taken
Where the fish grows with each new telling;
Another couple snuggles in open view
Whispering sweet nothings;
He tells her that he'll take her to Paris someday,
If they ever marry, or have the money—
—But probably not…
Yet another gaggle of three young women
Admire the figure of the lifeguard,
Whom we can only guess is
Too busy flexing to do his job;
But at least he'll have money by summer's end
For the new convertible everyone wants,
And a million other interactions
Happen on that beach,
But the young lovers only
Know their mutual intimacy.
They are safe in their bunker of sand;
Although they'll eventually leave
When the tide rises,
For now, they are safe.
Safe from the jokers and their sand baths,
Safe from the competition of the lifeguard
And his surface-deep godlikeness,
And safe from the prying eyes of other couples
In envy of their perfect enclave;
Here, they can talk
Of matters bearing all sizes,
Of their deep love,
And of things others dare not hear.
In a few hours,
Rowdy little boys will reclaim their hole,
But for now,
No one will want to
Intrude into the lovers' nest of sand.

THE OLD KIDS (THE LOVERS' NEST OF SAND, PART II)

An elderly man
Pushes an elderly woman
On a swing,
As each time back and forth
Ticks back, full-circle
To childhood,
When a younger man, then a boy,
Pushes a then-young girl on the same swing;
Laughing, pigtails swinging freely,
Little Gladys cried out:
"Don't push so high, George!"
The old man remembers
How the young boy of many decades past
Heeded the young girl's warning,
(In reality, the swing did not swing so high.)
And he slows down
So the giggling octogenarian
Sitting on the swing does not lean back
Too far, and if she did,
He has her, just as he did back then.
And in that moment,
On the kids' playground,
She's on the swing
And he's still pushing her gently,
While the young ones look on
At this old pair of geezers;
They wonder if their elders are senile, crazy, or both.
But these kids today are too grown up,
And the elderly celebrate youth.
So somehow,
Time stands still,
While age is rendered irrelevant;
Those old bones
Hold yet more youthful joy
Than anyone could guess,
But that's all that matters.
After all,
The passage of time brings pain,
And with that pain
We all secretly wish
We could laugh as that couple does:
Sitting on a swing,
We could enjoy living life, like the old kids.

EIGHT SMALL POEMS

• Chalkboard Poem

The chalk is white,
The board is black;
In a world out of whack,
It's a much different sight.

• Found in My Drawer

I found this poem in my drawer,
And one day I shall add some more,
—But not today, it's far too wet;
Plus, I don't feel like thinking yet.

• They Told Me

They told me I'm lazy,
They told me I'm crazy.
Now tell me:
If everything they said is true,
Then surely
They haven't yet spoken to YOU!

• Work Made Worthwhile

I had tried to do my work,
But alas, could not it seemed—
And I looked like such a jerk,
For my time was not redeemed.
Still, my time was hardly fruitless
Since my hobby was enjoyed;
So, you cannot say it's pointless
As I'm, in my fun, employed!

• Poetic Waste of Time

This poem was a waste of time,
Each word was just a waste of space;
There surely is a time for rhyme,
But clearly, here is not the place.

• Temptation

The world of temptation,
Through our own titillation,
Brings at first great elation;
But there's later damnation.

• Neglected Verse

If a poet can't write verse,
There is really nothing worse
That will ruin one's career,
And in time, I truly fear,
They neglect the very art
That they nourished from the start.

• Summer's Epitaph

The rain, it pours.
The wind, it blows.
Behind closed doors
I blow my nose,
And curse each leaf,
And curse the cold;
Oh why, cruel thief?
Where's summer's hold?

LEAVES UPON A BOUGH

Nineteen little leaves
Upon a bough,
There used to be twenty,
One less now—

And the green turns into red,
And the yellow now is brown,
All throughout the twinkling town
In my head—

And so, as the fall wears on,
All the leaves are falling down,
'Till the colors all but drown
Out each lawn—

I'm so happy I can see
All this beauty to behold;
Such a scene cannot be sold,
Not by me…
No, it shan't be sold by me.

A RANT, RHYMED

No matter how much you protest
All the reasons that I should detest
Every stupid thing you said in jest,
Just remember: You messed with the best.

No matter how much we agree,
All the answers are so plain to see;
Since the moment I saw I was free,
Far from you, that's where I'd like to be.

No matter how bad it's become,
As I'm living here under your thumb,
You will probably think this is dumb;
So why don't you shut it, old chum?

I'm starting to bore of my rant
On a problem the size of an ant,
And my patience is growing quite scant;
So, there's not much more time I can grant.

I'm not going to let you win;
Where you've lost, I won't even begin.
Now this speech is so long, it's a sin:
So be gone, lest I knock off your chin!

THE STORY OF SNEEZING SAM

There was a man named Sneezing Sam:
He sneezed so hard, he broke a dam!
And water gushed both to and fro,
'Till there was nowhere left to go;

The water rose to hide each roof,
And fill each boot and soak each hoof,
So every man and beast in town
All faced this fact: They may well drown.

They all cried out in one loud voice,
"Such woe, that we should bear no choice!
That Sneezing Sam is worth our scorn;
We'd all be dry, were *HE* not born!"

The townsfolk formed a mob, hell-bent
On making sure away Sam went–
But Sam, ashamed of his great sneeze,
Now tried to quell the town's unease:

He sneezed again a mighty gust,
So all the water soon was thrust
Away, and with the danger past
That Sneezing Sam, he sneezed his last.

AN ODE TO MY VOICE (Inspired by Lucille Clifton's "HOMAGE TO MY HIPS")

My voice
Is a strong voice
And it can make itself heard if it wants to;

My voice
Is a versatile voice
And it can sound like his, or hers, or yours, or theirs;

My voice
Is a sensual voice
And it caresses its words the way a lover caresses their beloved;

My voice
Is a different voice
And it has no interest in conforming to what it "should be";

My voice
Is a confident voice
And it won't hesitate to point out when others have the wrong ideas about it;

My voice
Is a powerful voice
And it can silence a room of other voices with one single utterance;

My voice
Is a beautiful voice
And it can sing like an angel or bewitch like a devil;

My voice
Is a persistent voice
And it will only stop speaking when it has said what it means to say;

My voice
Is a truthful voice
And it will not lie for the sake of gaining favor with corruption;

My voice
Is a worthy voice
And it has just as much right to be heard as anyone else's voice;

My voice
Is a faithful voice
And it will not hesitate to speak up or speak out for that in which it believes;

My voice
Is a unique voice
And it will not be replaced or silenced or drowned out by any allegedly "better" voices;

My voice
Is not a perfect voice
But it makes no apologies to anyone for how it sounds when it speaks;

Most of all,
My voice is my voice.
It is not your voice, or his voice, or her voice, or their voice.

And it will keep speaking until other people have thoroughly listened.

THE NEXT ROOM

Beyond the dank and dusty gloom
That rots as in a dead man's tomb,
Where apparitions tend to loom—
There, it waited: THE NEXT ROOM.

In front, there stood a man named Mars;
His head so tall, he scraped the stars.
And when he spoke, I filled with doom—
Thus, he warned me of the next room:

"You ought not, son, to go in there;
Its contents are too much to bear.
Back through that door you'll likely zoom—
DO NOT go into the next room."

More curious I grew at that,
And though I did not stay to chat,
I vowed return; then I'd exhume
The mystery of the next room...

Soon, back I came to end my quest;
I plucked my courage up to test—
But Mars returned! His wrath abloom,
He threw me into the next room!

So there I've stayed, as you might think,
And oft in madness walked the brink
Of daring that I might assume
You'd join me here...in the next room.

NINE POEMS IN MINIATURE

• Blight the White

I'm writing these words
Just to fill up this space:
And then, when I'm done,
There will not be a trace
Of a white space in sight,
That is not without blight

.

• Two Angels

Two angels stand, both side by side
To make the gulf of sin less wide,
So on your path you shall be safe;
As you walk on, you walk in faith.

• Double Standard

When you have a double standard
Where each choice can make you lose,
You must first reject BOTH options,
Then, create your OWN good news!

• Only for Today

If you find you cannot write,
Take it easy; do not fight:
Please don't lose your head, okay?
This is only for today!

• Rhyme of Endurance

I wrote this rhyme for nothing more
Than hoping that I might explore,
How much can just one verse endure?
Well, it's not much, I can assure.

• Writer's Block at Half Past Ten

This rhyme I wrote at half past ten
Was off to a good start, but then
There came a case of writer's block:
Thus ends my writing...quite ad hoc.

• One Ripple

When you feel betrayed and lonely

And you've had all you could take,
Just remember, this is minor;
It's one ripple in life's lake.

•   **Is This a Poem?**

Some call this a poem, but others do not;
Whatever it is, I guess I forgot.

•   **The Clipped Poem**

This verse was a quatrain
That was merely clipped in twain!

LEFT BEHIND

I'm tired of not "getting it,"
Pretending I'm not sweating it,
While trying, failing, losing, hating;
Now I'm just regretting it.
Living in my head,
Bound and beaten 'till I've bled,
What's the reason I keep trying it?
Must I be left for dead?

I won't stand to be undermined.
I have strength that you'll never find.
You need to make up your mind;
Better get on board, or you'll be left behind.

It's truly quite despicable:
You think I'm not applicable
To gaining, winning, loving, living;
That is not acceptable.
Living in my grief,
For the same inane belief,
Does that make my view expendable?
I'm caught between your teeth.

I won't stand to be undermined.
I have strength that you'll never find.
You need to make up your mind;
Better get on board, or you'll be left behind.

(Spoken)
Will you step over the crack?
Or should I bust your sorry back?
If you've gone on the attack,
You must know that you're out of whack.

I won't stand to be undermined;
That's my strength that you'll never find.
You don't care but I don't mind,
Now I'm on board while you're behind.

I can never be undermined.
You might see if you weren't blind.
I've worn down this same old grind;
At least I can't say that I've been left behind.

IT WAS FOR YOUR OWN GOOD

You may have been told
To take others' advice,
While those others assured you
Their words would suffice.
Then, the truth will be told
When the timing is right;
Though the facts are confusing,
There's no need to fight.
You will have your needs met,
'Cause you misunderstood:
See this place of oppression?
It's for your own good.

If you heard this before,
You might hear it again;
They still say it today,
Though they said it back then.
And the people are new
In a world still unchanged;
Here, the logic is sound,
While the thought is deranged;
They will say that you shouldn't
When, clearly, you could:
Their reasons don't matter,
It's for your own good.

Just as I see it now,
I have seen it before
On the faces of teens
Caught inside private war,
In the eyes of the parent
That buries their kid,
And the lives of the dead
In their graves where they hid,
As their bodies went cold
And as stiff as the wood,
I am sure they were told:
"It was for your own good."

THE NAMELESS POEM
(SOMETHING NEW)

It's really quite a shame,
This new poem has no name.
It will never achieve fame,
And to me, that's really lame.

This is no good at all,
Way these words on paper fall,
Not responding to my call;
It seems I have hit a wall.

This work seems rather flat,
And it's more than simply that;
There's no content, depth, or fat,
So the rhyme is tit for tat.

This verse has gone off track;
It's because I'm out of whack.
Now you must think I'm a quack!
For a purpose I do lack.

My thoughts have gone askew,
Thus, there's no more I can do,
And ideas are rather few;
So, I'll just write something new.

I MIGHT CRY

Here I am,
Alone in the crowd,
Anything but proud
Ready to burst this dam
Building up in my mind;
These paper friends,
Laminated bookends
Can't break the bind
Of feeling alone;
Give me a chance to be heard,
Just say the word,
And I'm drenched to the bone
With passive aggression,
Over how there's no sign–
Not your life on the line
Living with depression;
But it doesn't mean a thing,
'Cause it's not your issue,
More than one tissue
Needed to mend my broken wing:
Pay no heed
To the loss of intent
That once fueled my descent
To the depths of my need–
I'm done with this lie!
You can't see that I can't
Go on with this rant;
If I do, I might cry.

ANTICIPATE THE ROAD TO COME

Another chapter meets an end,
But still, I'm leaving with a friend.
I know not where from here I'll go,
But elsewhere; that is surely so.

I've had some laughs, yes, even tears;
But still, I've overcome my fears.
With time has come a wisdom grand
To guide my steps; it helps me stand.

How quickly it has come to this,
That I receive the future's kiss
Of confidence to boldly stride;
Toward reaching goals, I shall abide.

I'll leave behind my foolish quest
Of finding tools to manifest
The silly things I once held dear:
These are no more, I must make clear.

So, leaving hindsight in the past,
Where last week's issues fade so fast,
I look with eager eyes ahead,
My worried thoughts now put to bed.

The time runs short and days are few,
With sights to see and things to do:
Yes, now I think I can, old chum,
Anticipate the road to come.

I'M LISTENING

The one who said that life's not fair
Must have their head in the air,
Too high to see the world below,
To know
The folks left behind;
They may as well have been blind
To the justice we can't find,
Because we're different,
Can't even vent
Without being wrong;
We don't belong,
At least that's what we've been told,
And it's growing old,
Along with how we must fit the mold,
But we're round shapes
Been forced into so many square holes
Meant for square tapes
Recording all the pain in our souls;
Communication, invalidation
Just broadening misrepresentation
About whom we are;
We can't get too far
Without being labeled,
Or disabled
By others;
The fathers and mothers,
Even sisters and brothers
Say they want to join in:
Don't they know that slander's a sin?
Do they get it?
Can we ever fit?
I guess not.
Meanwhile, I'm getting hot;
My anger toward each big shot
Burns enough to kill a bull elephant,
It's irrelevant
Because you call my words conjecture,
Skip the lecture
Mr. Know-It-All;
I'll never take the fall
I admit that I over-think,
But the fact is, your rules stink!
If you're willing to come clean,
I'm listening...as long as you can say what you mean.

KINDNESS HELD BACK

Stop me if you heard it before,
About the little guy who grew into more
Than a nuisance;
Such dissonance
That's what hope is made from,
And then some,
Since you need to have support;
If you want a retort
To the world's negativity,
Use some creativity,
And you can have some positivity.
You might see you're not alone.
Get off the phone
With thoughts of being second-rate;
It's not your fate.
Only haters want to hate!
Who are you inside?
No one ever denied
That you can still try
Not to cry
When they lie;
If they want you to die,
Put your fist up!
There's no holdup
In trying to overcome
The mass of dumb
That says there's only one way
Or the highway;
There's something you can say,
And you'll send them away
With just one word;
We've all heard their side
But the world is too wide
For reality
To only be
Something the majority denied;
Don't compromise,
Or even worse, accept the lies.
Look in my eyes,
And see I'm being honest

When I say I believe
I'm right, but not self-righteous.
So I tell you, go achieve
That fuzzy win-it-all ending,
And we'll begin mending
All our kindness held back, because we need to be lending.